woven
wire
jewelry

woven wire jewelry

Contemporary Designs and Creative Techniques
including PMC techniques

Linda L. Chandler and
Christine R. Ritchey

INTERWEAVE PRESS

Editor: Judith Durant

Photography: Joe Coca and Lloyd Ritchey

Process photography: Linda L. Chandler

Photo styling: Paulette Livers

Cover and interior design: Paulette Livers

Production: Samantha Thaler and Dean Howes

Copy editor: Stephen Beal

Proofreader and indexer: Nancy Arndt

INTERWEAVE PRESS, INC.

201 East Fourth Street

Loveland, CO 80537-5655 USA

www.interweave.com

Printed in Singapore by Tien Wah Press (Pte) Limited

Library of Congress Cataloging-in-Publication Data

Chandler, Linda L., 1946-
  Woven wire jewelry : contemporary designs and
  creative techniques / Linda L. Chandler and Christine Ritchey.
      p. cm.
  Includes index.
  ISBN 1-931499-57-8
  1. Jewelry making. 2. Wire craft. I. Ritchey, Christine, 1951-
II. Title.
  TT212.C453 2004
  745.594'2--dc22
                                    2004005545

10 9 8 7 6 5 4 3 2

acknowledgments

LINDA THANKS

My students, who have been my inspiration and, at many times, my teachers. You know who you are!

My loving, supportive, and dedicated partner, Christine Ritchey, the guardian angel who has been essential to the quality of the finished book. Without her this book would not have been possible.

Christine's husband, Lloyd Ritchey, who has been the voice of reason and Christine's motivator.

My devoted and loving husband, Bud Chandler, who supports me in all my wishes, hopes, and dreams. He also made most of my tools and fixed everything that broke.

My son, Travis Chandler, who built my computer and keeps it running.

My mother, Corean Higdon, who brought me food when I forgot to eat.

And finally and especially, my wonderful daughter, Shane René Workman, who is my best friend and toughest critic. Who was there whenever I needed help. Who made decisions when I couldn't, gave wonderful advice, and taught me how to say no.

CHRISTINE THANKS

Linda Chandler, my funny, kind, and generous-to-a-fault co-author and teacher. The wonderful designs in this book are completely her own creations. I'll never understand how you get your ideas. Without you, there would be not have been a book to write.

My Interweave Press "family." Betsy Armstrong, for knowing a good thing when she saw it; for her guidance, advice, humor and, at times, psychotherapy. Judith Durant, for her great editing, for making me laugh and for her comforting e-mails when I was feeling stressed. Christine Townsend, Linda Stark, and everyone else at Interweave for their hard work. All of you have made me look much better than I really am.

My husband, Lloyd F. Ritchey, whose expertise and experience as a writer have been indispensable. Thank you for helping me to dream larger dreams and for pushing me in all the right directions. Thank you for your patience, support and love; and thank you for putting up with a total absence of home-cooked meals, a dirty house, and a moody wife. I love you so very much.

Tim McCreight, for his thorough review of the PMC projects, his editorial suggestions, his up-to-date information in new formulations of PMC, and his glowing praise that graces the cover of this book. Tim, you ROCK.

Rio Grande, especially Diana Montoya, who has given so much of her time during the writing of the book. Thank you for the tour of Rio, and for your unfailing support.

Jack O'Brian, President of Artistic Wire, for his sage advice and for sending me all the beautiful wire. I owe you a bracelet, at the very least. May you have many happy years of golfing.

contents

introduction

Angels can fly because they take themselves lightly.
—G. K. Chesterton, 1874–1936

"Adults" are at a severe disadvantage when it comes to taking up a new hobby or learning new skills. Sometime between when we are born and the time we reach "adulthood," we learn not to believe in magic. We learn to be self-conscious and judgmental of others and ourselves. "Adults" and "adulthood" are in quotes for the very good reason that we do not, in truth, ever grow up. We are just children with more work, less time, and more responsibility.

This book is not intended to be a textbook and, in the most important sense, should not be taken seriously (except for the parts about safety). This book is about having fun. Most importantly, it is about *playing*—like a child with a plastic bucket on the beach. The shells come to shore and bear the sound of the ocean inside. Everything is a wonderful surprise when it's looked upon with the eyes of a child.

So put on your child's eyes and play! Jewelry making is fun. You get to buy new toys and make pretty things out of sparkly stuff. In this book, we make mistakes and we show them to you. Mistakes are great teachers and many "mistakes," such as Silly Putty, the Slinky, and Post-It Notes turn out to be a lot of fun—and profitable as well. Don't worry about ruining your precious metals; there are many refiners who will take your messed-up metal and give you either money, credit, or new metal (see Resources at the end of the book).

If you don't like something about a project in this book, please change it to suit yourself. You will not be graded on your work. If a bolt of creative lightning inspires you, as we hope it will, go for it. How many people have accomplished something wonderful and said that they never would have tried if they'd known it couldn't be done? Try to keep that nasty word "can't" out of your vocabulary. "Can't" is the destroyer of creativity. We have tried to encourage creativity in this book. If we have accomplished that, then we will have achieved what we consider our most important goal.

So, leave all that judgmental, can't-do-it, isn't-good-enough thinking behind as you read this book and make the projects—or your own versions. Come inside and let's play!

safety

Making jewelry is not as dangerous as racecar driving, but there are hazards involved. The two most important tools in jewelry-making safety are common sense and self-awareness. If you are preoccupied or distracted, you run a big risk of injury.

This book assumes a basic knowledge of soldering. If you are a complete beginner, please get a copy of Tim McCreight's *The Complete Metalsmith* (Sterling Publishing, 1991). It's an inexpensive, spiral-bound book with lots of good advice and sound, basic techniques. (The companion video is great too.) Soldering requires the use of pickle, which is an acid. Soldering also requires some kind of torch. Torches use gasses, some of which are heavier than air. These gasses can ignite or explode if you don't take proper care to check for leaks. Read all manufacturers' literature and follow their advice.

SAFETY ESSENTIALS

1. Jewelry making requires good ventilation to keep your lungs safe from fumes and dust, and to prevent the accumulation of gasses.
2. Good lighting is necessary to prevent eyestrain. You can't make good jewelry if you can't see what you're doing.
3. A neat workspace will lessen your chances of knocking things over, especially chemicals and acids.
4. Wear safety glasses at all times to prevent eye injury from flying metals and acids. Soldering at high temperatures can also damage the retina of the eye, much the same as staring at the sun. Wear tinted safety glasses while soldering to lessen the amount of light that enters the eyes.
5. Wear a respirator to protect your lungs from metallic dust and fumes.
6. Be aware of your fingers at all times. Keep them away from acids and other caustic substances. You can easily cut yourself while using a flexible shaft or drill.

Clear safety glasses.
Safety glasses protect your eyes from flying metal pieces and splashes from the pickle pot, among other unexpected hazards. These should be worn from the minute you enter your workshop until you leave. Please don't take chances with your eyes.

Grinding and buffing machines have claimed the lives of several careless fingers.

7. Tie back long hair. Ironically, it is better not to wear jewelry while making jewelry.

8. If you have pets, keep them out of your workspace. Young children need supervision, and you won't be able to divide your attention adequately, while in your studio, between your children and your work. Make sure you can work without fearing for children's safety and jeopardizing your own. Do not allow children in your studio and lock the studio door when you leave.

9. Always keep a fire extinguisher in the studio and a bowl of water on your worktable. When you're soldering on charcoal blocks, keep a spray bottle of water nearby. The blocks can smolder for a long time, so make it a habit to spray water on them before you leave the studio unattended.

10. Many jewelry-making processes require you to sit for long periods of time while you saw, hammer, and solder. We don't want to find you crouching in a bell tower playing the lead role in *The Hunchback of Notre Dame*! Stand up and walk around at least once an hour. Stretch your body forward and backward and side-to-side. Squeeze your hands into tight fists and then open your hands and spread your fingers as widely as possible. Rest your eyes by looking at something in the distance. Arrange your workspace so you can work comfortably, without having to hunch over or strain in any way. Try to maintain good posture.

These warnings should not alarm you. They are meant to make you aware of the hazards inherent in jewelry making, and obeying them will become habit in a very short time. Remember to use your most important tools—common sense and self-awareness.

tools and
equipment

This chapter shows some of the essential tools you'll need to complete all of the projects in this book. You will use these tools to cut, twist, form, and shape wire and sheet metal. Many of the tools can be found at a hardware store. For suppliers of jewelry tools and equipment, please see the Resources chapter.

Quick-Grip clamp

The Quick-Grip clamp is a simple, spring-loaded clamp that is used for every weaving project in this book. Almost any clamp with straight, soft jaws will do.

If it's necessary to use a clamp with metal jaws, wrap the jaws with masking tape. Clamps are available at hardware stores.

Stepped/chain-nose pliers form loops

Pliers and cutters

Pliers and cutters are the basic tools of jewelry making. A good assortment includes *flat-nose, round-nose, and needle-nose pliers, plus wire cutters.* Pliers are used for holding and shaping wire.

Flat-nose pliers for bending wire

Cutters for cutting wire

Pliers and cutters are used so much that they are usually the first tools to break, so purchase the best you can afford. Many people believe pliers made with a box-joint last longer (the catalog description should tell you if the pliers have a box joint). Look for pliers that have a comfortable grip. It is not unusual to become devoted to your favorite pair of pliers.

Stepped/chain-nose pliers are used for forming curves and circles. Most of the clasps in this book are made with these pliers.

Needle-nose pliers for gripping and bending wire

Round-nose pliers for curving wire

Nylon-jaw pliers for jobs that require the wire to be unmarred

Cutting and smoothing tools

1. Bench vise with clamp and anvil. The vise clamps onto your worktable and is very useful for holding projects steady. The anvil is used for hammering and forming.

2. Jeweler's saw. The jeweler's saw is an essential part of any jewelry maker's tool kit. The saw is used to cut shapes out of sheet metal and to cut through heavy wire. You will find yourself picking up this saw again and again.

1

2

3. Bur Life saw lubricant. Never try to saw without lubricant—the result will be much frustration and lots of broken saw blades. Beeswax is a good lubricant as well.

4. Hand file. The large hand file is used to remove metal quickly. You can move an uneven bezel back and forth across its surface to make the bezel perfectly flat.

3

4

5

5. Needle files. Needle files come in flat, round, triangular, and many other shapes and are used to smooth and shape your work. The most essential files are a flat file and a round file.

More cutting and polishing tools

1

1. Steel scribe. Scribes are used to mark sheet metal for cutting, drilling, and measuring.

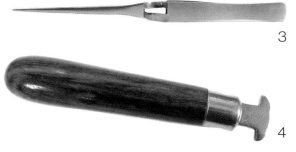

3

2. Straight-blade shears. Shears are useful for cutting out metal shapes and making solder chips. Another great cutting tool to have is a pair of Joyce Chen scissors. These are found in gourmet kitchen shops. They will cut most gauges of sheet metal with little effort (and with a lot of effort will cut a penny in half!). Accept no substitute; get the original.

4

3. Stainless steel precision tweezers. Tweezers are used to pick up small gems and hot metal. They are also handy for placing tiny solder chips. You'll find that tweezers are useful for many things.

4. Steel bezel roller. The bezel roller is used to press bezels around stones and gems by using a rocking motion. The bezel roller is often called a bezel rocker for this reason.

2

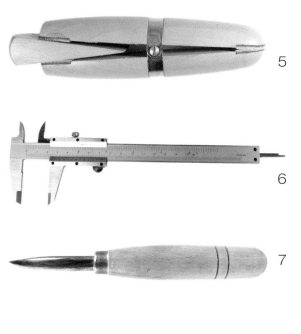

5

5. Ring clamp. The ring clamp is used to stabilize rings while they are being worked on. We use it to hold objects for sawing.

6. Caliper. Calipers are used to measure the thickness of wire and sheet metal. They are also indispensable for measuring all that stock you ordered and forgot to mark! There are many kinds of calipers to choose from. Try to purchase a caliper that has both inches and millimeters.

6

7. Burnisher. The burnisher is used to shine (burnish) metal and compress porous metals, such as PMC, in preparation for soldering.

7

8. Bench knife (not pictured). Any penknife or pocket knife will work. We use the knife in many of the projects to lift and separate metal.

Metal shaping tools

1. Rawhide mallet. This mallet is used for jobs requiring that the metal not show hammer marks, such as shaping a ring on a ring mandrel.

1

2. Chasing hammer. This hammer is used for any light job that needs a good whack, such as work-hardening a piece of wire or sheet metal.

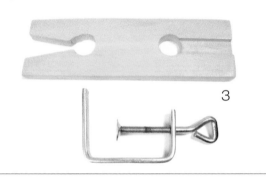

2

3. Bench pin. This attaches to your bench or worktable. The wooden bench pin provides a surface for sawing and piercing sheet metal. The wooden pin can be bought as a flat piece and shaped according to your needs, or purchased with a deep V pre-cut into the wood.

3

Opti-Visor

Opti-Visor or other magnifying device. This visor is so necessary that many jewelers walk around with one on their heads and forget to take it off!

Safety soldering glasses

Green-tinted safety glasses are necessary when soldering at very high temperatures, as with platinum. The high temperatures used in soldering platinum can burn the retina of the eye, much the same as staring at the sun. The disadvantage is losing the ability to see the color of the metal as it is heated.

Soldering tools and equipment

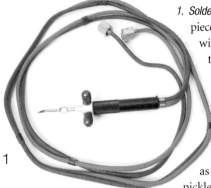

1. *Soldering torch.* The photgraph shows the hoses and hand piece from a Little Torch. Gas tanks and gauges are used with this torch. If a less expensive torch is desired, try the Bernz-O-Matic torch. This is a simple acetylene canister with a four-foot hose and one tip and should be adequate for most of the projects in this book.

2. *Pickle pot.* Jewelry is placed in the pickle pot after soldering to remove firescale (oxidation). We advise using a small Crock-Pot as a pickle pot. It's inexpensive and has a lid. (Once the Crock-Pot has been used for pickle, it should never be used for anything else.)

3. *Pickle (not pictured).* This usually comes in the form of powder which is mixed with distilled water. This forms an acid solution that is added to the pickle pot. When it's time to change the pickle, neutralize it by adding baking soda. This will create a somewhat alarming fizz and a noxious smell. When the fizzing stops, add a little more baking soda. If fizzing begins again, you need to add more baking soda. When there is no fizzing, the acid has been neutralized and is safe to pour down the drain. Gardeners sometimes dilute the pickle and pour it on acid-loving plants, such as azaleas. An alternative to conventional pickle is sodium bisulfate, sold at swimming pool supply stores as "ph-down" and other names. This is sometimes cheaper and works just as well. Always use copper tongs to place your piece in the pickle and to remove it.

4. *Flux.* A definite must-have, it helps prevent the oxidation, or firescale, that occurs when soldering, and also helps the solder melt. Plain old borax mixed with distilled water or denatured alcohol also works well as a flux.

5. *Third Hand with locking tweezers.* This is a wonderful tool used to hold work while soldering and performing other tasks. Sometimes you'll feel like even three hands aren't enough!

6. *Paintbrush.* Any small paintbrush can be used. These are great to use in PMC work, and to apply flux and pick up solder chips when working with metals. Always have several paintbrushes handy.

7. *Charcoal block.* These are great for soldering, and we use them frequently in the projects. You can make them last longer by wrapping stainless steel binding wire around the edges. A cheap alternative is soft firebrick. These can be found in ceramic supply stores and sometimes hardware stores. Use a hacksaw to saw the brick into slices to make several soldering surfaces. Wear a dust mask while sawing these bricks.

8. *Solder pick.* This tool is used to pick up heated solder. It's also handy for chasing solder chips around and putting them back in place. Solder chips have an annoying tendency to wander off when flux turns liquid from heating.

Flexible shaft and accessories

The flexible shaft machine is a very useful tool. You can live without it—for a while. It is very much like the drill used in the dentist's office. The flex-shaft tool drills, sands, forms, and polishes much faster than files and sandpaper wielded by hand. The handpiece allows precise control and the foot pedal (not pictured) leaves both hands free.

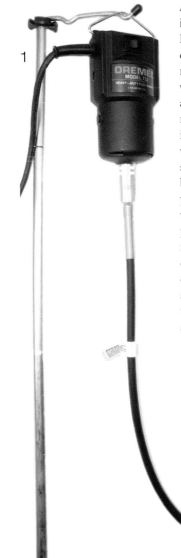

A good flex-shaft is an investment. Foredom and Dremel, among others, produce good flexible shaft machines. If your budget won't stand the purchase of a flexible shaft machine, a regular Dremel Moto-Tool is a good compromise. It will accept all the accessories, just like a flex-shaft, but has no foot pedal, so you must control the speed with one hand. Dremel products can be found at most hardware stores. Foredom products are purchased through jewelry supply catalogs. Please see the Resources section for suppliers.

1. Flexible shaft motor. The flexible shaft usually comes with a stand, handpiece, and foot pedal.

2. Polishing disks. These disks attach to your flexible shaft machine. The different disks are used to cut, rough-polish, and give a final polish to sheet metal and wire.

3. Drill bits and other assorted cutting and drilling tools. These attach to the flexible shaft machine and are used for drilling, forming, and finishing sheet metal.

4. Assorted burs. Burs fit onto your flex shaft and are great for texturing and drilling shapes into metal, and for stone setting.

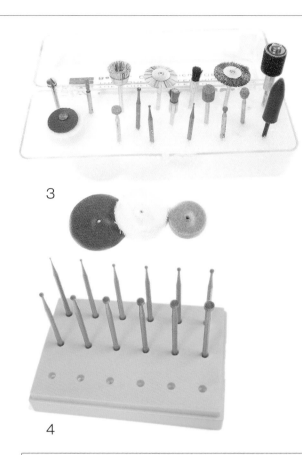

3

4

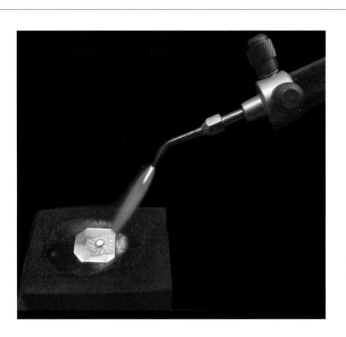

Torch
The Smith Little torch in action.

Tumbler

This is the same tumbler used for polishing rocks. In jewelry making, the tumbler is used, along with steel shot and a polishing liquid, such as Sunsheen, to polish jewelry. The steel shot knocks off any rough places and makes the metal shine.

There are two kinds of steel shot. Carbon steel shot is cheapest, but it does rust. Stainless steel shot is more expensive, but almost maintenance-free. We recommend stainless steel mixed shot, which has a variety of shapes to polish every tiny place on your jewelry.

The polishing solution must be changed and the shot rinsed when the solution starts to look gray. If you put a pretty piece in the tumbler and it comes out a horrible, dull gray (seeing results like this can almost make you pass out), just change the solution, rinse the shot, and re-tumble the piece.

wire weaving techniques

Practice is the best of all instructors.
—Publilius Syrus ~ 100 B.C.

Most of the woven projects in this book—complex neckpiece and simple bracelet alike—use the same techniques and tools. Some patterns may look complicated, but they're all based on a fairly simple weaving process. Before you tackle the actual projects, we suggest that you make the practice piece described on the following pages. After teaching many weaving classes, we have found that making such a piece helps students master the weave with ease and success. Once you learn this basic weave, you can create even more involved and intricate designs.

Materials	Tools	
20- or 22-gauge (0.8 mm or 0.6 mm) round dead-soft sterling silver wire. (Since this is only a practice piece, you can use inexpensive copper wire from the hardware store if you wish.)	Clamp (we use a Quick-Grip clamp from the hardware store) Needle-nose pliers Flat-nose pliers Stepped/chain-nose pliers (these are not absolutely necessary, but they sure do help)	Nylon-jaw pliers Wire cutters Masking tape Ruler Sharp-pointed felt marker Opti-Visor or some other magnifying device Patience—LOTS of patience!

Figure 1
Wires taped.

Figure 2
Wires in
the clamp.

Figure 3
Push first set
toward you.

GUIDELINES

❖ Mark your clamp on one side. This will be the front side, and the mark should always be facing you. If you need to put down your weaving to answer the phone (or get the cat out of the fireplace), you'll always know which side you should be working on.

❖ Use a soft cloth to clean and straighten each wire. Fold the cloth over the wire and pull the wire gently but firmly through the fold.

❖ Always work from right to left.

❖ A set means a group of wires—usually two or three wires per set.

❖ Concentrate on maintaining a consistent tension on the wires throughout the weaving process. Consistency will ensure that the final piece has straight, even edges.

❖ When you're cutting wire, remember to wear safety glasses and hold the wire on both sides of the place you are cutting. Doing so will prevent injury from flying parts.

PROCEDURE

Cut eight pieces of wire 10" (25.5 cm) long. Clean and straighten each wire. Align the wires evenly and tightly together and keep them flat. Wrap tape around one end of the group of wires to keep them together (**Figure 1**).

Place the taped end in the clamp. We've used a red dot to mark the front. This mark should always be facing you (**Figure 2**).

Separate the wires into sets of two, pushing the first set toward you and the second set away from you (Figures 3 and 4). Alternate the sets until all four sets are lying even with or below the clamp.

Figure 4
Push second set away from you.

You should have two sets bent toward the front of the clamp and two sets bent toward the back (Figure 5).

Make sure the sets are even and close together. Always work from right to left.

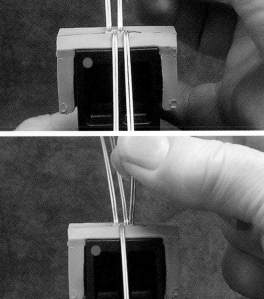

Figure 5
Two sets bent forward and two sets bent back, even with the clamp.

Bring the first set straight up and gently pull it through your thumb and forefinger several times (Figure 6). This stroking motion will increase your control by helping straighten the wires and work-hardening them.

Figure 6
First set straight up.

Bend the first set across the other sets to the left of the clamp (Figure 7). Make sure that the right wire of this set is lying directly on top of the left wire.

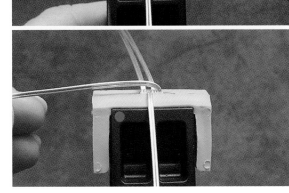

Figure 7
Bend first set to the left.

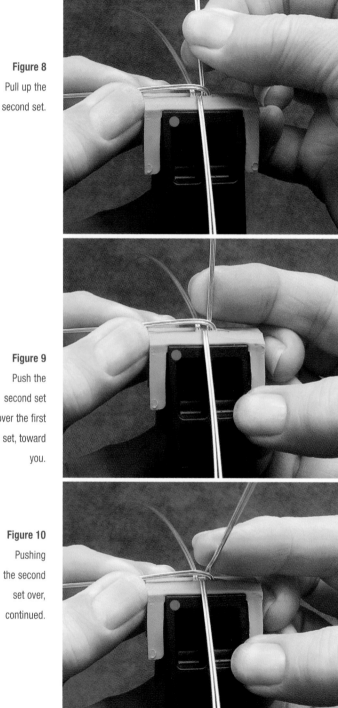

Figure 8
Pull up the second set.

Figure 9
Push the second set over the first set, toward you.

Figure 10
Pushing the second set over, continued.

If necessary, pinch the wires with needle-nose pliers to help keep them parallel. Hold this set between the thumb and index finger of your left hand while you work with the other sets.

Always work close to the clamp. Make sure you are holding the wires parallel with the top of the clamp, and not at an angle.

Take a moment to make sure the first set is lying as closely as possible to the other sets. Pushing this first set over with your finger may help.

Now bring the second set straight up and pull it through your fingers as you did with the first set (**Figure 8**).

Push the second set over the first set toward you, using your index finger (**Figures 9 and 10**). Use just enough pressure to make close contact with the first set. Don't press so hard that you force the wires of the first set out of position.

Continue pushing the second set over, making sure you have a very close fit against the first set beneath (**Figure 11**). Your wires should be straight, even and close together (**Figure 12**).

Continue weaving by bringing the third set up, over and down, this time pushing it *away* from you toward the back of the clamp (**Figures 13 and 14**).

Figure 11
The second set pushed over.

Figure 12
Check wires for straightness.

Figure 13
Pushing the third set toward back of clamp.

Figure 14
The third set pushed to the back of the clamp.

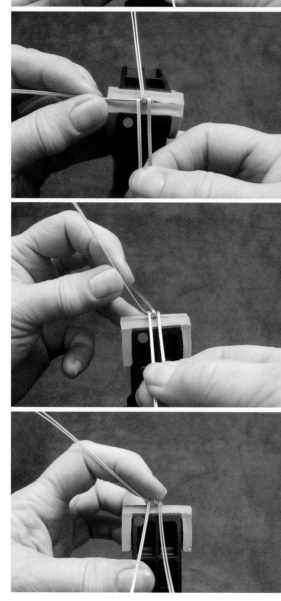

Figure 15
Push the fourth
set toward
the front of
the clamp.

Figure 16
Wires straight,
even, and
close together.

Figure 17
Bending up
the first set.

Figure 18
Loosen the
clamp and
press down on
top of the piece.

Push the fourth set toward you and toward the front of the clamp (**Figure 15**).

Check once more that your wires are straight, even and close together (**Figure 16**). If the wires need adjusting, move them into the correct position with needle-nose pliers.

Take the first set that you've been holding between your left thumb and index finger and bend it up just slightly (**Figure 17**).

Loosen the clamp and press down firmly on top of the piece until the first row is down inside the clamp, then retighten so the first row is held in place (**Figures 18 and 19**).

Pull the first set straight up and through your thumb and index fingers as before (**Figure 20**). Ensure an even edge by keeping this set as close as possible to the next set.

Hold this set in your right hand. At the same time, push the set to the back of the clamp with the index finger of your left hand (**Figure 21**).

You should now have two alternating sets on either side of the clamp (**Figure 22**). This completes the first row. Take a moment to make sure the sets are straight, even, and close together.

To begin the second row, lift up the second set, now on the far right (**Figure 23**).

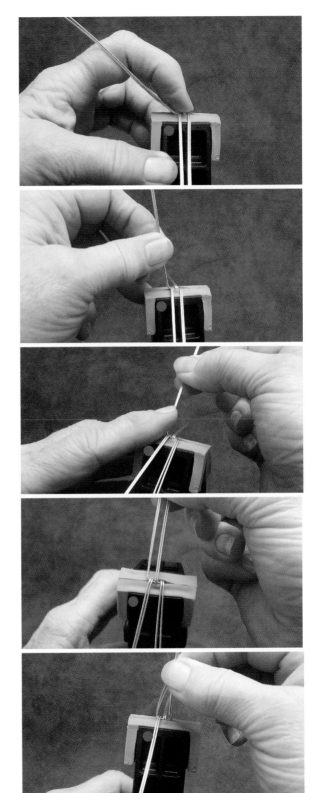

Figure 19
The first row pushed down and held in place by the clamp.

Figure 20
Pulling up the first set.

Figure 21
Pressing the first set to the back of the clamp.

Figure 22
The first row completed.

Figure 23
Second row. Lift the second set.

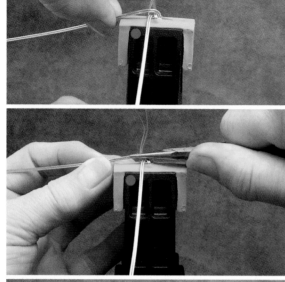

Figure 24
Bringing the
second set
across to
the left.

Figure 25
Help from
the pliers.

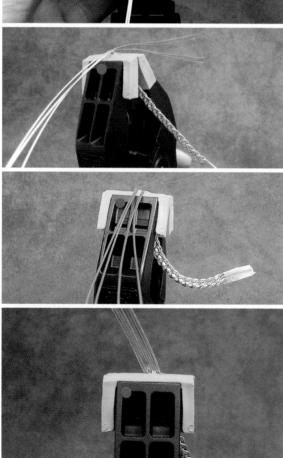

Figure 26
The piece will
feed through
the right side
of the clamp.

Figure 27
Woven too
tightly on the
right side.

Figure 28
Pull the end
wires together
and straighten.

Make another row in exactly the same way you made the first (**Figure 24**).

Remember to maintain consistent tension on the wires throughout the entire piece. If you have problems bringing a set across, use pliers to help put the set into place (**Figures 25**). As you work, the wire becomes easier to manipulate.

After you've completed several rows, you will notice that the piece is exiting through the right side of the clamp. The weave is actually on a diagonal course (**Figure 26**).

Keep working with this practice piece until weaving feels natural to you and your piece shows straight sides and even rows.

Figure 27 shows what happens when the weaving is too tight on the right side—the woven piece is curling from the tension. A similar problem can occur if the set that has been brought across to the left of the clamp is held at an angle and not parallel to the top of the clamp. Usually, the piece can be saved simply by bending and straightening the weave.

Finish by pulling the end wires together and straight (**Figure 28**). Flatten the wires with pliers, then cut off close to the woven section (**Figure 29**).

The woven piece will have a ridge running down the middle that you can flatten with nylon-jaw pliers (**Figure 30**).

Do the Math

After you've completed a few weaving projects, you'll want to get creative. Good! Go for it! Remember that you must have an even number of sets, or the border of your bracelet will be uneven. For example, say you decide to use three wires per set instead of two. You decide to use twenty-one wires. Will this work? Twenty-one (wires) divided by three (wires per set) equals seven sets. This won't work because you'll have seven sets of wires, which, of course, is an odd number. Something's got to change. You could use eighteen wires because eighteen (wires) divided by three (wires per set) equals six. Voila! An even number! You'll have three sets on either side of your clamp.

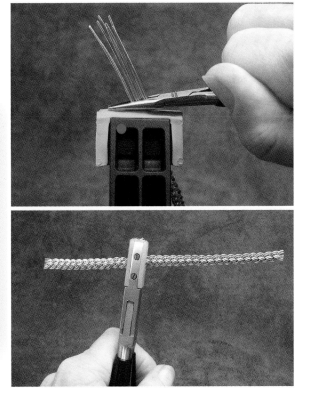

Figure 29
Flatten with pliers, then cut off.

Figure 30
Flatten the weave with nylon-jaw pliers.

A Few Tips

Always weave with dead-soft wire. Since the wire is handled so much during weaving, it will always become work-hardened. If you start with half-hard or hard wire, the work-hardening will make the wire impossible to work with, and the wire could even break.

Sterling silver is preferable to fine silver for weaving. Sterling has more spring to it and a memory for its shape. Fine silver is much too soft. After you have worked with silver, try using other materials. Gold-filled wire makes a beautiful bracelet. Try combinations of copper and silver. Colored copper wire, such as Artistic Wire, has many design possibilities. Try the wonderful niobium colors. One caveat for colored wire: Use nylon pliers, or tape the jaws of your regular pliers. This will keep the color from scratching off.

It is very helpful to maintain a record of your weaving projects as a guide for future projects. Save any scrap wire in a container to be returned to a metal refiner in exchange for credit, cash, or more wire. Be sure not to mix types of wire; for example, put only sterling silver in one container and gold-filled in another.

the woven bracelet

Start by doing what is necessary, then what is possible, and suddenly you are doing the impossible.
—St. Francis of Assisi

This beautiful bracelet may look complex, but it's actually fairly easy to make. Start cultivating your best Mona Lisa smirk so you can use it later when people admire your new creation and ask how on earth you made it!

Materials

22-gauge (0.644 mm) round, dead-soft sterling silver wire for the woven piece

12-gauge (2.05 mm) half-round, half-hard sterling silver wire for frame (If transferring a decorative pattern to frame, use dead-soft sterling silver instead of half-hard.)

16-gauge (1.29 mm) half-round, half-hard sterling silver wire for the wire wraps. (If transferring a decorative pattern to wire wraps, use dead-soft sterling silver instead of half-hard.)

12-gauge double half-round, sterling silver wire for the clasp

Tools

Needle-nose pliers

Flat-nose pliers

Round-nose pliers

Stepped/chain-nose pliers (not required, but helpful)

Nylon-jaw pliers

Ring clamp

Jeweler's saw

Saw lubricant

Flat file

Wire cutters

Masking tape

Ruler

Sharp-pointed felt marker

Opti-Visor

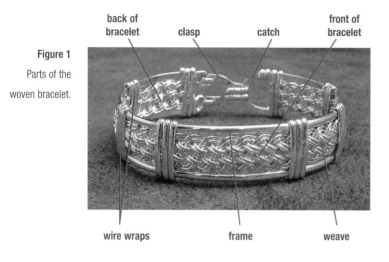

Figure 1

Parts of the
woven bracelet.

back of
bracelet

clasp

catch

front of
bracelet

wire wraps

frame

weave

MAKING THE WOVEN BRACELET

The project consists of the woven part of the bracelet, the frame, and the clasp. As with all the chapters, please read through the entire project before beginning.

Note: If you want to impress a decorative pattern into the frame or wrap wire (see instructions on page 26), add the following to your list of tools: coarse sandpaper, patterned brass sheet or similar material to use as a pattern source, and a rawhide mallet or bench vise to hammer or squeeze the pattern into the wire.

ANATOMY OF A WOVEN BRACELET

Major parts of the woven bracelet are shown in Figure 1. *Note:* The front of the bracelet is the part that faces out; the back of the bracelet is the part worn against the wrist.

You will be weaving with six sets of wire instead of the four sets you wove in the practice piece.

Cut twelve wires 10" (25.5 cm) long (six sets of two wires), which will make a bracelet for a 6 to 6½" (15 to 16.5 cm) wrist. Just as in any type of weaving or knitting, everyone will weave slightly looser or tighter, so the length of wire you cut will depend on the tension of your weave. Make adjustments in wire length if you would like a larger or smaller bracelet. As a general rule, take the length you want to weave and add 3" (7.5 cm). Refer to the instructions for the practice piece as needed.

Clean and straighten each wire. Weave as in the practice piece until you have a woven piece a little over 6" (15 cm) long (**Figure 2**).

Figure 2

Woven piece.

Cut off the unwoven wires at both ends of the weave with wire cutters, making your cuts even and straight across. You must have 6" (15 cm) of weave to fit a 6 to 6½" (15 to 16.5 cm) wrist.

MAKING THE FRAME

Now we'll make a wire frame for the bracelet. The wire for the frame must be long enough to encircle the woven piece and form a clasp. With the woven length being 6" (15 cm), double that figure and add 3" (7.5 cm) more. This will make the half-round wire 15" (38 cm) long, which should be more than enough to make the frame. It is always better to have a little extra length than too little. Clean and straighten the wire.

Pick up the half-round wire at its midpoint (7½" or 19 cm) with flat-nose pliers (round side of wire facing toward you) and bend the wire down with your fingers (**Figures 3 and 4**).

The wire may try to curve the wrong way, and you want the round side of the wire facing toward you at all points. If this is a problem, straighten the wire with pliers placed across the curved end (**Figure 5**).

Keep bending the wire until it forms a U-shape to fit the woven piece. Use the pliers to refine the U-shape to fit the woven piece closely (**Figure 6**).

The U-shaped end of the frame will become the catch. Leave a space about ⅜" (1 cm) between the weave

Figure 3
Pliers at halfway point.

Figure 4
Bending the wire.

Figure 5
Pliers across the curved end to straighten.

Figure 6
Squeeze frame to fit the woven piece.

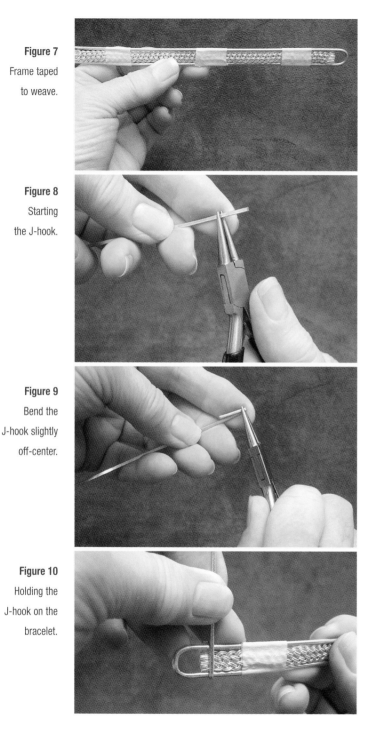

Figure 7
Frame taped
to weave.

Figure 8
Starting
the J-hook.

Figure 9
Bend the
J-hook slightly
off-center.

Figure 10
Holding the
J-hook on the
bracelet.

and the catch end. The open end of the frame will become the clasp end. The frame wires at the clasp end should extend about ¾" (2 cm) beyond the weaving. Measure and mark the center and 1" (2.5 cm) from each end of the woven piece with a felt marker. Wrap the marked places with masking tape (**Figure 7**).

MAKING THE WIRE WRAPS

If you want to impress a pattern into the wrap wire, place it flat-side down on a rigid, flat surface. Cover the wire with the sandpaper or other patterning material (we used a brass patterned sheet, which is available from jeweler suppliers [see Resources]), and hammer evenly with a rawhide mallet. (You could also use a bench vise or a rolling mill to squeeze the patterning material against the wire.)

We'll place eight sets of wire wraps around the frame to hold the bracelet together. As you wrap, the bracelet will start to actually look like a bracelet, and each successive wrap will be easier than the one before. Be patient with yourself if you've never done this before. Lots of detail is given in the next few pages to help you become an accomplished wire wrapper.

Cut about 6" (15 cm) of half-round wire for the first wrap. Every wrap starts with the J-hook. The first J-hook is a little longer than for the other wraps; the extra length will be wrapped around the side of the catch.

Hold the wire with the flat side toward you and grasp it with the very tip of the round-nose pliers about ½" (1.3 cm) from the end. Your palm should be facing up (Figure 8).

Roll your hand to the left until the back of your hand is facing up. Bend the J-hook a little off-center, to the left (Figure 9).

Slide the J-hook onto the bracelet with the short end of the J-hook on the back (flat side of the frame wire). Apply pressure against the bracelet with the third and fourth fingers of your left hand to hold the two pieces together (Figure 10). This leaves your right hand free to manipulate the pliers.

Important: Make sure that the short part of the J-hook is slanted toward the catch, and always wrap from left to right. The front (rounded side of the frame wire) of the bracelet should have straight, vertical wraps and the back side should have slightly slanted wraps. Each wrap must slant in the same direction.

Squeeze the J-hook into place with the needle-nose pliers (Figure 11). Start the wrap about ¼" (6 mm) from the end of the woven piece. Later, we will slide the wrap to the left so it covers the exposed wire ends.

Reposition the pliers to hold the bracelet and the wrap wire at the same time (Figure 12). Use your left index finger to push the wrap wire snugly over the top and toward the back of the bracelet (Figure 13).

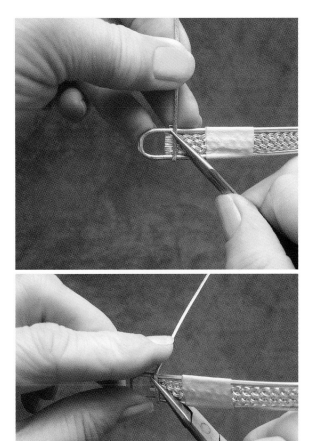

Figure 11
Squeeze the J-hook into place with pliers.

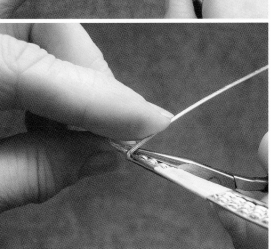

Figure 12
Reposition pliers.

Figure 13
Push wire to the back.

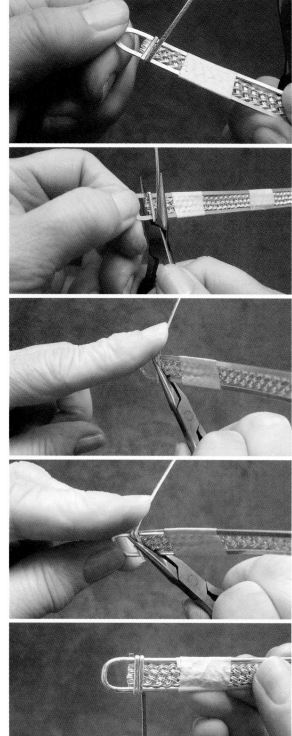

Figure 14
Back side of bracelet.

Figure 15
Press wire down with the pliers.

Figure 16
Hold bracelet and the wrap wire with pliers.

Figure 17
Push wrap wire over the top and toward the front.

Figure 18
Front side. Two wraps finished.

Turn the bracelet to the back and press the wire firmly into place with your pliers—*not with your finger* (**Figures 14 and 15**).

Hold the bracelet and the wrap wire with the pliers and use your left index finger to press the wrap wire over the top and toward the front of the bracelet (**Figures 16 and 17**).

Turn the bracelet to the front and use the pliers to press the wrap into place (**Figure 18**).

After completing two wraps, use your pliers to slide the wraps over the unwoven wires (**Figures 19 and 20**).

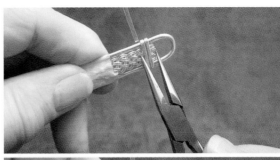

Figure 19
Slide the wraps
to cover the
unwoven wires.

Figure 20
Unwoven wires
covered.

Bend the short end of the wire twice around the catch (**Figures 21 through 24**).

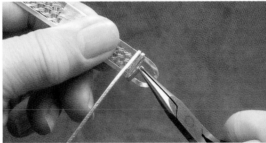

Figure 21
Back side.
Lift short end
of the wire.

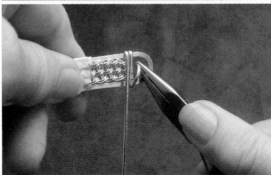

Figure 22
Back side.
Curve the
wire through
the catch.

Figure 23
Back side.
Pull the wire
through.

Figure 24
Front side. Continue wrapping wire around frame.

Figure 25
Back side. Cut and file wire.

Figure 26
Press wire firmly against frame.

Figure 27
Front of bracelet.

Figure 28
Back side before cutting the long wire.

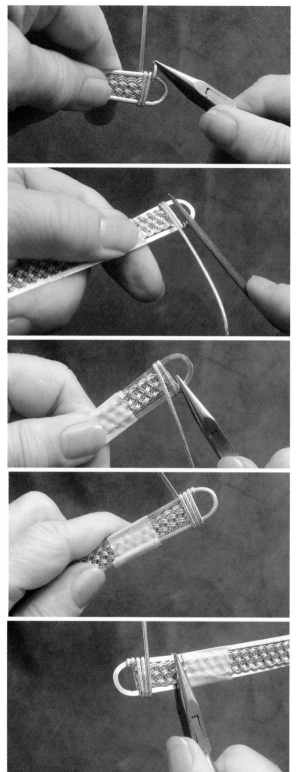

The second wrap should end at the back of the catch. Cut off any excess wire and file the cut end until it is perfectly smooth (Figure 25). Any rough spots would make wearing the bracelet uncomfortable.

Press the filed end firmly into place against the frame (Figure 26).

Take the long end of the wrap wire and make another wrap. The front of the bracelet should have three complete wraps (Figure 27).

Figures 28 and 29 show how the back should look before and after cutting the long end of the wrap wire. Cut the wrap wire to depth of frame.

File the cut end and press it firmly into place with your pliers. You are finished with this end.

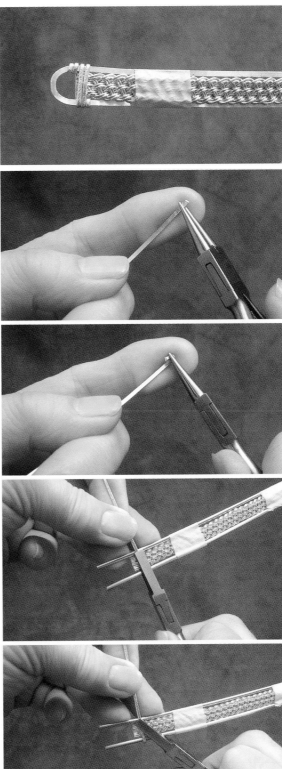

Figure 29
Back side after cutting wire, filing, and pressing the wire into place.

Figure 30
Make a shorter "hook."

We will now work on the clasp end. Cut another 6" (15 cm) length of wire and use round-nose pliers to make a J-hook with a shorter "hook" than the first one (**Figures 30 and 31**).

Figure 31
J-hook completed and bent off-center as before.

After making the J-hook, place it on the bracelet as before. Wrapping this end is a bit difficult; the frame will try to move out of alignment, and the wrap wires have an annoying tendency to slip off the end. Use flat-nose pliers for better control (**Figure 32**).

Figure 32
Squeeze wrap wire firmly into place.

Start your wrap a bit farther back from the end of the weave than you did on the catch end. Hold the wrap wire and the frame firmly with your pliers and push the wrap wire over the top of the frame and toward the back (**Figures 33 through 35**).

Figure 33
Hold wrap wire and frame firmly with pliers.

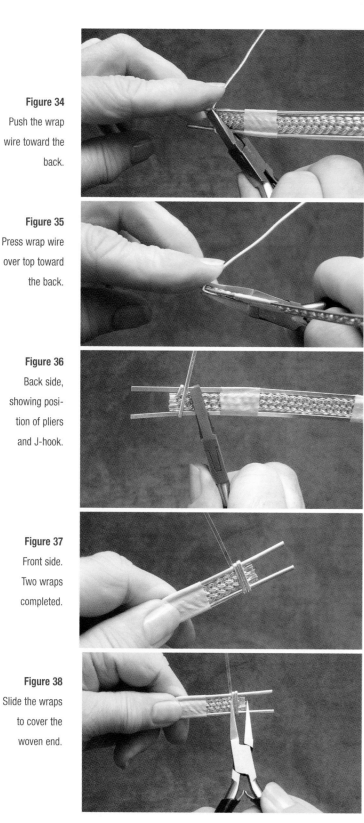

Figure 34
Push the wrap wire toward the back.

Figure 35
Press wrap wire over top toward the back.

Figure 36
Back side, showing position of pliers and J-hook.

Figure 37
Front side. Two wraps completed.

Figure 38
Slide the wraps to cover the woven end.

Do not wrap so tightly that the frame is squeezed out of alignment. After the wraps are in place, you will be able to go back and tighten them.

Notice the pliers holding the frame firmly and the position of the J-hook (**Figure 36**).

Complete two wraps (**Figure 37**) and use the needle-nose pliers to slide the wraps toward the end to cover the unwoven wires (**Figures 38 and 39**).

If this wrap seems to want to slip off the end of the bracelet, use your pliers to bend the ends of the frame out slightly.

Complete this end with three wraps of wire on the bracelet front (**Figure 40**).

Cut the wrap wire about ¼" (6 mm) long on the back side, file the wrap end smooth, and press firmly into place with your pliers. **Figure 41** shows the finished back side with the wraps in place.

Remove the masking tape from the ends and clean with a product such as Goo-Gone, acetone, or fingernail polish remover. Leave the middle of the bracelet taped and tape as needed while you complete your wraps.

Measure ¾" (2 cm) from the end of your finished wraps and mark with a felt pen. Start the next wrap here and repeat on the other end.

Work back and forth, measuring, marking, and wrapping. Remember to file each end after cutting. Once you have four wrap sets, as in **Figure 42**, you can place your next four wraps farther apart if you wish.

Try spacing your wraps 1" (2.5 cm) apart, always wrapping one end and then the other. Most people find that leaving a larger space in the middle is more attractive.

Figure 43 shows a common problem for those new to wire wrapping. You can see that the wrap is uneven. This happens to experienced wire wrappers as well, and usually happens at the beginning, when the J-hook is put into place.

One way to cure this problem is to make your J-hook longer and cut and file it later. This wastes wire, but it does work. The preferable method is to lift the wire with a penknife as in **Figure 44**. Lift the wire until you can grasp the end with your pliers.

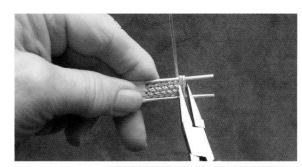

Figure 39
Woven end covered by wraps.

Figure 40
Front side finished with three complete wraps of wire.

Figure 41
Back side finished.

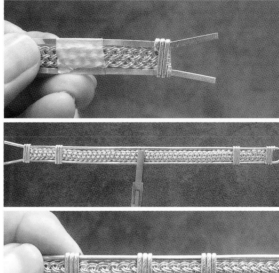

Figure 42
Front of bracelet with four completed wraps.

Figure 43
Front side of bracelet showing an uneven wrap that needs adjustment.

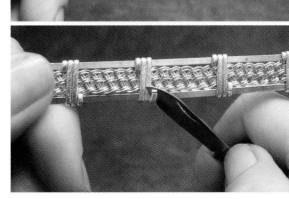

Figure 44
Back side of bracelet. Lift the end of the wire with a penknife.

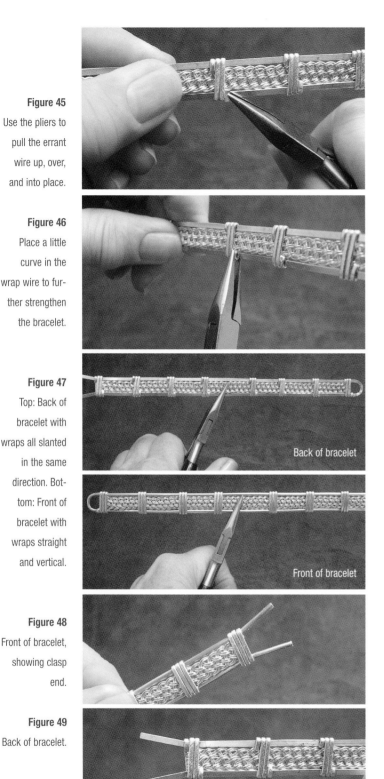

Figure 45
Use the pliers to pull the errant wire up, over, and into place.

Figure 46
Place a little curve in the wrap wire to further strengthen the bracelet.

Figure 47
Top: Back of bracelet with wraps all slanted in the same direction. Bottom: Front of bracelet with wraps straight and vertical.

Back of bracelet

Front of bracelet

Figure 48
Front of bracelet, showing clasp end.

Figure 49
Back of bracelet.

Pull the wire up and over and into place (**Figure 45**). When you are comfortable with wrapping the bracelet, you may want to try curving the very end just enough to allow it to dig into the weave. This will further strengthen the bracelet, but is not absolutely necessary (**Figure 46**).

Figure 47 shows both sides of the bracelet. Notice that all the wraps on the back side are slanted in the same direction, with the ends of the wraps cut and curved into the weave. Run your finger across each wrap to check for smoothness. There should be no rough spots. If there are, then lift the offending wrap end, file until smooth, and press back in place with your pliers. The wraps on the front side should be straight and vertical.

Figures 48 through 50 show how the ends of the bracelet should look at this point. The clasp end should have the frame wires spread slightly to prevent the wrap from slipping off (**Figure 49**).

MAKING THE CLASP

Use needle-nose pliers to twist the frame wire so the flat side is facing inward and the round side is facing outward (**Figures 51 and 52**). Do this on both sides, close to the beginning of the wrap. Remember that the clasp end should measure about ¾" (1.3 cm). Use either stepped/chain-nose pliers or round-nose pliers to grasp the very end of one of the frame wires and begin to roll it down and inward (**Figure 53**). After you have rolled the wire about halfway into a circle, reposition your pliers and complete the curve (**Figure 54**). Repeat on the other wire.

After both frame wires are rolled down (**Figure 55**), cut a piece of double half-round wire 1½" (3.8 cm) long. Place it in a ring vise at the halfway point.

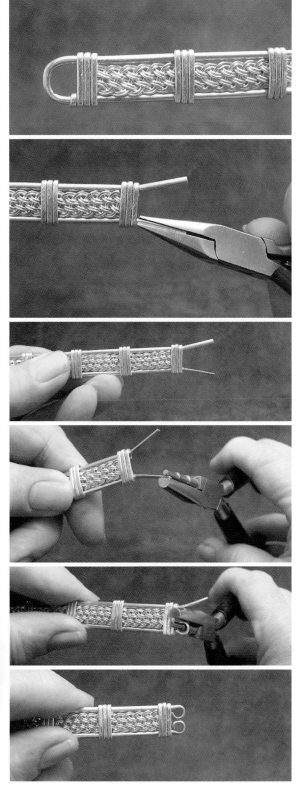

Figure 50
Front of bracelet. The catch end should look like this.

Figure 51
Use needle-nose pliers to twist the frame wires so the flat sides of the wires face the inside.

Figure 52
Frame wire turned toward inside.

Figure 53
Roll wire inward.

Figure 54
Reposition the pliers and complete the curve.

Figure 55
Both wires rolled down.

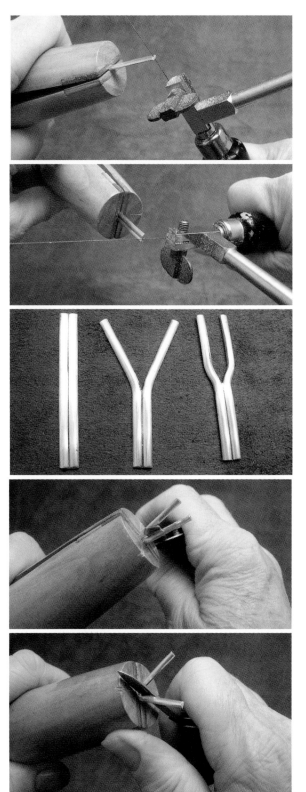

Figure 56
Saw down the middle of the double half-round wire.

Figure 57
Same thing, different view.

Figure 58
Left to right: wire sawed to the mid-way point, spread apart, and shaped into what will become the clasp.

Figure 59
Use a penknife to separate the sawed wires.

Figure 60
Use the penknife to separate the legs into a V-shape.

Use a jeweler's saw to cut down the middle of the wire (**Figures 56 and 57**).

Remember to lubricate the saw blade with a product such as Bur Life or beeswax. Your saw blade will break very easily without lubricant.

Figure 58 shows the wire at different stages as it is formed into a clasp.

When you have sawed through the wire to the halfway mark, leave the wire in the ring vise and use a pen knife to separate the wires (**Figure 59**). Now that the double half-round wire is cut in half, we will refer to the wires as "legs."

Move the penknife from side to side until the legs form a V-shape (**Figure 60**).

File inside the legs with a flat file to make the edges smooth, and keep filing to make the legs a little thinner. The thinner legs will fit more easily inside the loops you made in the frame wires (**Figure 61**).

Figure 61
File inside of the wires to smooth and thin them.

Place your needle-nose pliers about ⅛" (3 mm) from the bottom of the V and bend the leg until it is parallel with the unsplit part (**Figures 62 and 63**). Repeat on the other leg. The finished piece will resemble a tuning fork.

Figure 62
Place pliers ⅛" (3 mm) from bottom of the V.

Figure 63
Straighten wire.

Check for fit (**Figures 64 and 65**). If the legs are spaced too widely for the loops, squeeze them together slightly with your pliers. If the legs are too close together, spread them slightly.

Figure 64
Both legs straightened. Check for fit with the loops at the end of the bracelet.

Figure 65
The legs fit nicely through the loops.

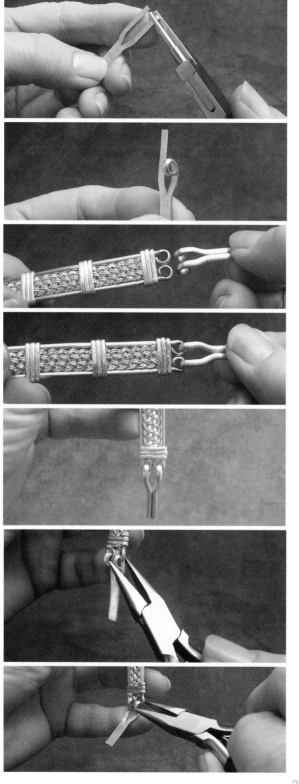

Figure 66
Grasp the end of one leg and begin to roll it down.

Figure 67
One leg rolled down.

Figure 68
Both legs rolled down and ready to check for fit.

Figure 69
Checking for proper fit.

Figure 70
The clasp should hang straight down and move freely.

Figure 71
Use the pliers to press the loop closed.

Figure 72
Bend the ends of the loops into a more circular shape.

Measure from the bottom of the V and cut off the legs to about ¾" (2 cm). File the cut ends until they are smooth.

Use round-nose or stepped/chain-nose pliers to grasp the end of one leg and begin to curl it down (**Figure 66**).

Make sure to roll the flat side over so that the round side stays on the outside.

Roll the legs down until they are almost closed, but leave enough room to slip the clasp onto the loops at the clasp end (**Figures 67 and 68**). Reposition your pliers as needed.

Attach the clasp to the loops (**Figure 69**). The clasp should move freely and hang straight down when you lift the bracelet (**Figure 70**).

File the front and back of the bracelet's clasp-end loops if necessary to make them thinner and improve the fit. It may be necessary to file the clasp legs as well to ensure a proper fit.

Use needle-nose pliers to gently press the loops on the legs closed (**Figure 71**). Reposition the pliers to press the ends down into a more circular shape (**Figure 72**).

Now turn your attention to the other end of the clasp. Use wire cutters to nip off tiny pieces until you have roughed out an oval-shaped end (Figure 73).

Using a flat file, refine the oval shape until you are pleased with the way it looks. This end should blend nicely to form the rest of the clasp and have no rough spots (Figure 74).

Use stepped/chain-nose pliers or round-nose pliers to make a small upward curve at the very end of the clasp (Figure 75). Make sure the round side of the clasp is turned up.

Reposition the pliers about ⅛" (3 mm) from the end of the clasp and begin to roll the end of the clasp down. The round side of the wire is on the outside and the flat side is on the inside of this curve. You always begin a curve with your palm facing up and roll by turning your hand over.

Figures 76 through 78 show the progression and completion of the clasp. Reposition the pliers as necessary.

Figure 73
Cut sharp corners off to rough out an oval-shaped end.

Figure 74
Use the file to refine and smooth the end.

Figure 75
Make a slight upward curve at the very end of the clasp.

Figure 76
Begin rolling the wire down, and reposition the pliers as necessary.

Figure 77
The pliers are now on the second step, as the curve needs to be wider.

Figure 78
Finished clasp.

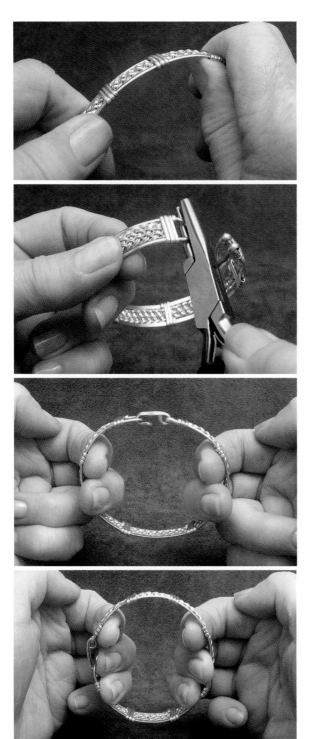

Figure 79
Begin curving the bracelet with your fingers.

Figure 80
Curve the catch slightly downward.

Figure 81
Close bracelet and pull the sides into an oval shape.

Figure 82
Gently pull the clasp side and the opposite side apart.

SHAPING THE BRACELET

Once the clasp has been completed, begin curving the bracelet with your fingers (**Figure 79**). Keep bending until you have a smooth, slightly oval shape. You want an oval shape that will conform to your wrist—no one has a round wrist.

Use either stepped/chain-nose or round-nose pliers to curve the catch down slightly. This will help the catch and clasp to connect more easily (**Figure 80**).

To further refine the shape of the bracelet, connect the clasp to the catch. Use two fingers on either side of the bracelet and pull the bracelet into a more oval shape (**Figure 81**). Turn the bracelet and put three fingers on the inside, against the clasp and the opposite side, and gently pull (**Figure 82**). These pulling motions will give the bracelet a nice, smooth appearance.

The bracelet is finished (Figure 83). Now check the operation of the clasp. Cup your hand behind the bracelet and push upward with the thumb while at the same time pushing inward from the top (Figure 84). The clasp should fall open from the catch (Figure 85).

The natural tendency is to push the open bracelet over the fingers and hand. Eventually, this can stretch the bracelet out of shape. Instead, spread the bracelet apart just enough to slide it onto the thinnest part of your wrist. Close the bracelet by again pushing the ends toward each other (Figure 86).

This bracelet is usually worn with the clasp on the bottom of the wrist. To remove the bracelet, push the catch and clasp toward each other until the clasp falls open. Remove the bracelet by opening it just enough to slide it off the thinnest part of your wrist.

For the finishing touch

Put the bracelet in the tumbler for eight to twelve hours. This will further work-harden the piece, get rid of any rough spots you missed, and give the bracelet beautiful shine and sparkle. We hope you will enjoy your bracelet for years to come.

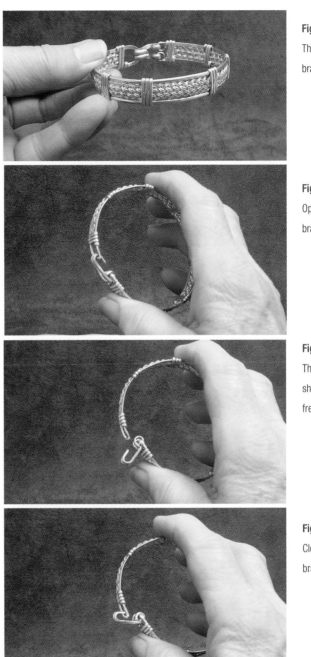

Figure 83
The finished bracelet.

Figure 84
Opening the bracelet.

Figure 85
The clasp should dangle freely.

Figure 86
Closing the bracelet.

a domed cuff bracelet
with soldered bead ends

*Whether you believe you can
do a thing or not, you are right.*
—Henry Ford (1863–1947)

This elegant bracelet is one of many variations of the woven bracelet in Chapter 4. Very fine wires are woven, the weave is domed, and the ends are finished with beads. Because doming makes the bracelet hug your wrist, there is no clasp to bother with, and the fine wires give the surface a beautiful sparkle.

Materials	Tools	
22-gauge (0.5 mm) dead-soft round sterling silver wire	Nylon-jaw pliers	Clamp
Two 12 to 14 mm Bali beads (or choose your own beads—just make sure they are sterling)	Needle-nose pliers	Charcoal blocks
	Flat-nose pliers	Flux
	Jeweler's saw	Easy solder
	Rawhide mallet	Stainless steel binding wire
	Rubber mallet Ring clamp	Wire cutters
	Saw lubricant	

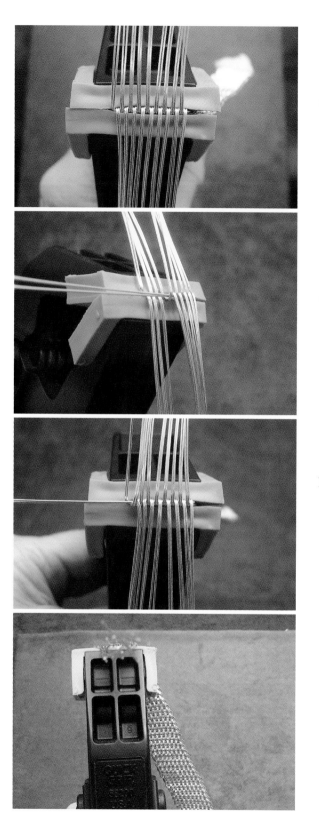

Figure 1
Wires in the clamp, straight and close together.

Figure 2
The right set brought across. The right set is very close to the other sets.

Figure 3
Top view of the first row, almost finished.

Figure 4
Almost through weaving. Wires must be kept straight.

Cut 36 wires into 10½" (26.5 cm) lengths, which should make a bracelet 6½" (16.5 cm) long. Use masking tape to tape one end of the wires, and place the them in the clamp.

This weave uses the same method shown in Chapter 3, but with eighteen sets of wires instead of four. Since you are using so many wires, it is especially important that they be kept straight.

Notice how close together the wires are in Figure 1. Figures 2–4 show progressive stages of weaving. Sets should be tight and close as they are folded over.

If the wires start to curve, each succeeding row will curve more than the one before. If curving occurs, unweave until you reach a straight row and try again.

After you have woven 6½" (16.5 cm), cut off any remaining wires (**Figure 5**).

Figure 6 shows the two mallets we will use to dome the bracelet.

Put the woven piece around the rubber mallet, letting the side of the weave hang about ¼" (6 mm) over the mallet edge. Tap the side of the bracelet with the rawhide mallet to form the weave into a domed shape (**Figure 7**).

Figure 5
The finished weave.

Figure 6
A small rawhide mallet and large rubber mallet.

Figure 7
Beginning to dome the bracelet.

Figure 8
Work back and forth, alternating sides.

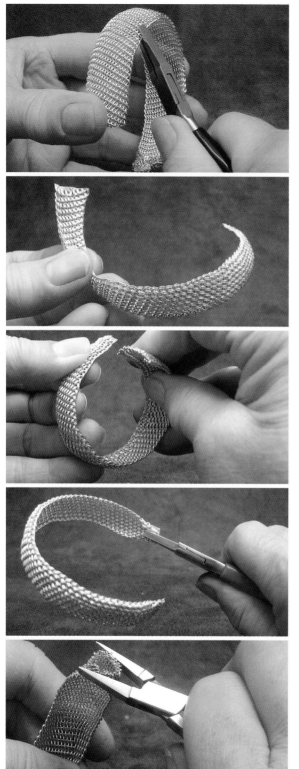

Figure 9
Use pliers to help bend the sides down evenly.

Figure 10
Curve the domed weave into a bracelet shape.

Figure 11
A nice bracelet shape.

Figure 12
Fold the ends toward the center.

Figure 13
Press the bent sides flat.

Work back and forth along one side then repeat on the other side. You may have to do this several times before you are pleased with the shape (Figure 8). You can use flat-nose or nylon-jaw pliers to help bend the sides down evenly (Figure 9). Bend the weave into a nice bracelet shape (Figures 10 and 11).

Use flat-nose pliers to fold the ends of the weave toward the center. You want the ends to be small enough to fit inside the beads (Figure 12). Press the bent sides flat against the back with pliers (Figure 13). Figure 14 shows both ends with sides folded over and pressed to the back.

Use stainless steel binding wire to further tighten the ends. Start by threading the binding wire through holes in the weave (Figure 15). Pull the binding wire tight and wrap the remaining wire around the end of the weave (Figures 16 and 17).

Figure 14
Both ends folded and pressed to the back.

Figure 15
Tighten with binding wire.

Figure 16
Wrap the binding wire around the end.

Figure 17
Binding wire wrapped tightly around the end.

Saturate both ends with flux and add little chips of solder to both ends of the weave (Figure 18).

Figure 18
End ready to solder.

Solder piece

Flux

Figure 19
Place charcoal so only the bracelet ends are showing.

Figure 20
The solder has not yet flowed.

Figure 21
The front of soldered ends before going into the pickle, binding wires removed.

Figure 22
The back of soldered ends before going into the pickle, binding wires removed.

Place charcoal blocks around the bracelet so that only the ends and a small amount of weave are exposed. Doing so will make it unnecessary to heat the entire piece (**Figure 19**).

Begin soldering by heating the woven part just above the charcoal. Keep the flame moving. When the woven part is almost red, move the torch to the end of the bracelet where the binding wire is.

Figure 20 shows that the binding wire and heat from the torch have darkened the silver. When the solder is ready to flow, the darkness should clear up and you should see a bright stream of silver.

If the binding wire gets soldered to the woven piece, it will peel off quite easily. In any case, remove the binding wire before you put the piece into the pickle pot (**Figures 21 and 22**).

It is important to let the piece *air-cool* to room temperature before you put it in the pickle pot so the piece will remain hard. If you were to quench the piece in water right after soldering, the piece would become soft.

TROUBLESHOOTING

If the solder doesn't flow, the flame may not be hot enough. If increasing the torch heat fails to make the solder flow, the piece is probably dirty. Clean the piece by putting it in the pickle pot. *Be sure to remove the binding wire before pickling the piece. Binding wire should never go in the pickle.*

When the piece is properly soldered and air-cooled, place it in the pickle pot for cleaning.

To prepare the Bali beads for soldering, place one of the beads in the ring clamp (**Figure 23**). If the bead is too wide, try putting the ring clamp wedge in the side of the clamp (**Figure 24**).

Cut off one quarter of the bead with the jeweler's saw (**Figure 25**). It's always better to saw off too little than too much. It's easier to start sawing if you form a groove in the bead with a couple of light strokes. You may also use a file to make a groove.

Keep your saw blade lubricated with beeswax or a product such as Bur Life (**Figure 26**). **Figure 27** shows the sawing progress.

Figure 23

The bead in the ring clamp.

Figure 24

A wedge in the side of the clamp to accommodate the bead's width.

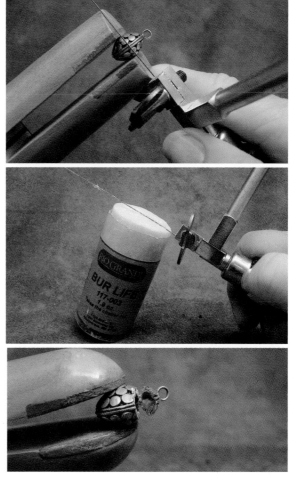

Figure 25

Saw off the first quarter of the bead.

Figure 26

Use lots of lubrication on the saw and use it often.

Figure 27

The bead end partially cut off.

Figure 28
Soldered ends ready to fit the beads.

Figure 29
Checking the bead for fit.

Figure 30
Thumbnail marks length of weave that went inside the bead.

Figure 31
Bead pushed onto the weave —a nice, tight fit.

Figure 32
Using nylon-jaw pliers to flatten the bead for a better fit.

Figure 33
Wrap silver wire around the end if the bead opening is too large.

Check for fit by pushing the bead onto the weave as far as possible. When you have pushed the bead on as far as it will go, place your thumb directly below the bead (**Figure 29**). Remove the bead, but keep your thumb on the spot you were holding (**Figure 30**). Your thumbnail will show how far the weave went into the bead. You want the bead to fit tightly on the weave and the weave to be inside the bead as far as possible (**Figure 31**).

Of course, you won't always be lucky enough to have the bead fit perfectly every time. If the opening is too large, flatten the bead for a tighter fit using nylon-jaw pliers (**Figure 32**). You can also make the woven end larger by wrapping it with sterling silver wire (**Figure 33**). If the bead opening is too small, place flat-nose pliers inside the bead and press outward to open the bead.

Figure 34

The front of the bracelet with flux and solder pieces added.

Figure 35

The back of bracelet. Place flux and solder pieces all the way around the piece.

Figure 36

The bead after soldering and pickling.

After you have a good fit, solder the bead in place. Saturate the woven end and the inside of the bead with flux and add small chips of solder. Push the bead onto the woven end and add more flux and solder chips around the weave where it meets the bead.

Figures 34 and 35 show flux and solder chips placed where the weave meets the bead, ready for soldering. Use the charcoal technique shown in Figure 19 when you solder. Let the bracelet air-cool as before, then put in the pickle pot to clean (Figure 36).

When you are certain the bead is tightly soldered to the weave, put the bracelet in the tumbler for several hours or overnight. Figures 37 and 38 show the bracelet after tumbling.

Figure 37

The front of the bracelet after tumbling.

Figure 38

Side view of the finished bracelet.

You're finished!

Remember to put the domed bracelet on the smallest part of your wrist. Never try to force the bracelet over your hand.

free-form bracelet

*The freedom to make mistakes provides
the best environment for creativity.*
—Anonymous

This bracelet is fun to make and begs to be customized. Once you understand the technique, you can try various combinations of wire and materials. For example, adding beads or wire coils to the long, curved parts can produce interesting results. The bracelet can be lengthened to make a great ankle bracelet or choker. You can wear it on your upper arm, Cleopatra-style. Maybe you will even invent a new weave! It might be a good idea to make this bracelet in copper until you master the technique.

Materials	Tools	
16-gauge (1.3 mm) round dead-soft gold-filled wire (This wire makes a strong bracelet that will hold its shape very well.)	Masking tape	Flat file
	Flat-nose pliers	Wire cutters
	Nylon-jaw pliers	Clamp
	Round-nose pliers	Ruler
	Stepped/chain-nose pliers	Sharp-pointed felt marker

Figure 1
Make a loop.

Figure 2
Wrap the loop
with masking
tape.

Figure 3
Taped wires in
the clamp

Figure 4
Wires
uncrossed and
straightened.

Figure 5
Wires divided
into three sets
of two wires.

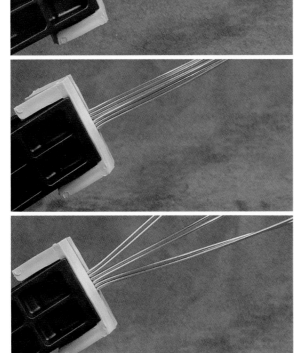

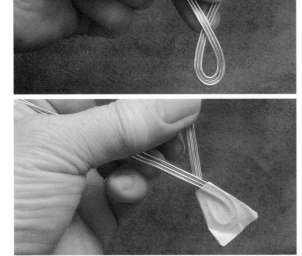

These instructions are for a 7" (18-cm) bracelet. The bracelet has seven sections that should measure about 1" each. To lengthen or shorten the bracelet, add or omit one or more sections.

Cut the wire into three 20" (0.5 m) pieces. Find the center and fold the wires in half with flat-nose pliers. The wires should form a loop that crosses in a graceful curve (**Figure 1**).

The loop's inside diameter should be about ½" (1.3 cm) at its widest part. Wrap this loop with masking tape (**Figure 2**) and place the taped loop in the clamp (**Figure 3**). Uncross the wires and straighten them (**Figure 4**). This may sound strange, but hang in there!

Divide the wires into three sets of two wires (Figure 5). We will call the sets the left set, the middle set, and the right set. As you weave, the sets will change position often. To avoid confusion, whichever set happens to be on the left will be called the left set, whichever set is in the middle will be the middle set, and whichever set is on the right will be the right set.

Move the middle set behind the left set (Figure 6). Complete the first twist by pulling the middle set to the left with your left hand and the left set to the right with your right hand (Figure 7). This twist should be fairly tight. Keep the wires flat and in line. Just let the clamp dangle.

Grasp the top of the twist with your left thumb and index finger and spread the wire sets farther apart to prepare for the second twist (Figure 8). To make the second twist, place the middle set behind the left set (Figure 9) and bring the left set in front of the middle set (Figure 10). Keep a tight grip on top of the first twist throughout these steps.

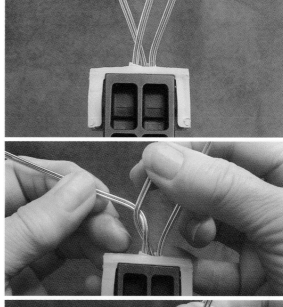

Figure 6
The middle set placed behind the left set.

Figure 7
Making the first twist.

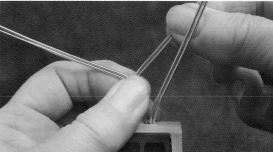

Figure 8
Hold the top of the twist very firmly and spread the sets far apart.

Figure 9
Place the middle set behind the left set.

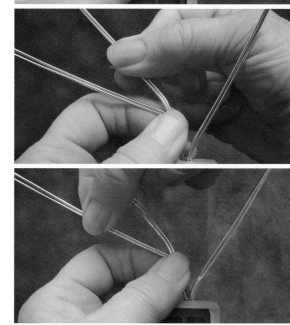

Figure 10
Place the left set in front of the middle set.

Figure 11
Completing the second twist.

Figure 12
The two twists completed.

Figure 13
Grasp the right set in your right hand.

Figure 14
Curve the right set and bring it behind the middle set.

Figure 15
The left set pulled across and in front of the other two sets. The intersection is circled.

Figures 11 and 12 show the completion of the second twist.

Bend the right set of wires to the left, behind the middle set, to join the left set (**Figures 13 and 14**). Try for a graceful curve.

Pull what is now the left set to the right, across and in front of the other two sets (**Figure 15**). Grasp the place where the wires intersect (marked by the circle). Place your left hand as in **Figure 16**. This completes the first section.

Measure here to make sure this section is about 1" (2.5 cm) long. If the section is much longer than 1" (2.5 cm), you have woven too loosely. Conversely, if the section is much shorter than 1", you have woven too tightly. In either case, it would be a good idea to start over. If your sections are only slightly off, just try to keep each section the same length. Remove the clamp.

For the second section, we will make the twists on the right side of the bracelet. Keep a tight grasp and spread the sets far apart. Bring the middle set to the right and in front of the right set (**Figure 17**). Now bring the right set to the left and behind the middle set (**Figure 18**). Figure 19 shows the first twist finished.

Bring the right set to the left, behind the middle set. Bring the middle set to the right and in front of the right set. **Figure 20** shows the two finished twists on the right side of the bracelet.

Figure 16
Grasp the intersection of the wires firmly.

Figure 17
Bring the middle set to the right and in front of the right set.

Figure 18
The right set goes to the left, behind the middle set.

Figure 19
The first twist finished.

Figure 20
The two twists are finished.

Figure 21
Curve the left set to the right.

Figure 22
Bring the left set in front of the middle set to join the right set.

Figure 23
Pull the left set farther to the left.

Figure 24
Pull the middle and right sets farther to the right.

Figure 25
Bring the middle set to the left behind the left set.

Figure 26
Bring the left set in front of the middle set.

Take the left set and make another graceful curve to the right and in front of the middle set to join to the right set (Figures 21 and 22). This process completes the second section.

Move the left set farther to the left and move the middle and right sets farther to the right to prepare for the third section (Figures 23 and 24).

At this point, you should begin to see a pattern emerging. The first section has two twists on the left and a curve on the right. The second section has two twists on the right and a curve on the left. Now you will simply repeat the first section and the second section until you have seven sections (or as many sections as you need for the length you desire). Remember to measure each section to make sure each is about one inch long.

To begin the third set, bring the middle set to the left and behind the left set. Bring the left set to the right and in front of the middle set (Figures 25 and 26).

For the second twist, bring the middle set to the left and behind the left set, and the left set to the right and in front of the middle set. This completes the two twists of the third set.

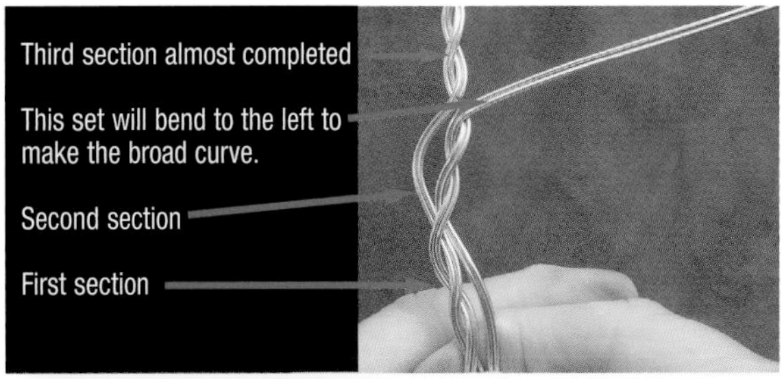

Figure 27 shows the progress at this point. You can see that the first section has two twists on the left and a long bend on the right. This is reversed on the second section, and the third section will be identical to the first section when you make another graceful bend from right to left to complete the third section (Figures 28 and 29).

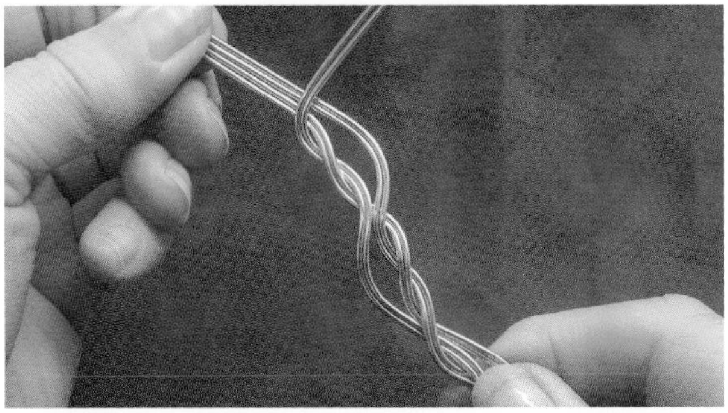

Note that on the odd-numbered sections, the curve goes *under* the middle set and on the even sets the curve goes *over* the middle set.

Curve the bracelet slightly in the direction of its final shape. This helps the wires lie flat and makes the whole process easier. Every section will alternate between having one set on top and two sets on top (Figure 30).

After making the last section, cross the left set across the other sets to the right (Figure 31). Use flat-nose pliers to hold the two sets in place

Third section almost completed

This set will bend to the left to make the broad curve.

Second section

First section

One set on top

Two sets on top

Figure 27
Reviewing the process.

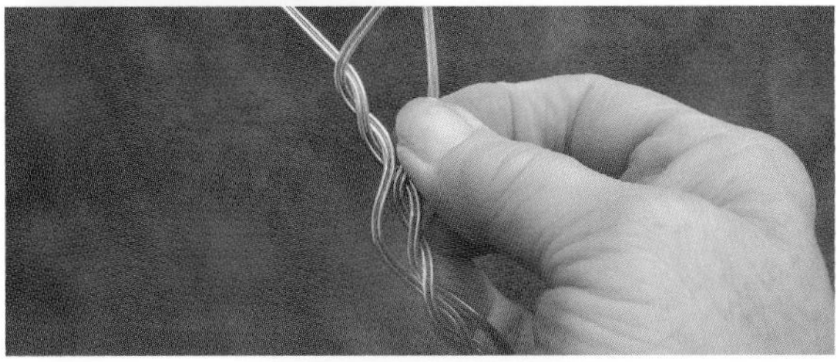

Figure 28
Make a curve to the left with the right set.

Figure 29
The third section completed and ready for the fourth section.

Figure 30
One set on top; two sets on top.

Figure 31
The last section.

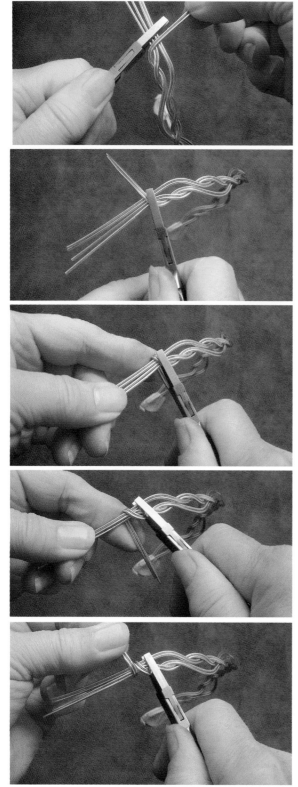

Figure 32

Beginning to wrap the end of the bracelet.

Figure 33

Hold the set with pliers to make wrapping easier.

Figure 34

Wrap to the back.

Figure 35

Bring the wrap around to the front.

Figure 36

Making the second wrap.

(**Figure 32**) while you begin to wrap the left set tightly around and to the back of the two right sets. Now hold the wires as in **Figure 33** while you continue wrapping the left set around the other two sets.

When you have wrapped the wires to the back, tighten the wrap securely with pliers (**Figure 34**). This end will ultimately hold the bracelet clasp.

Make one more wrap by bringing the left set to the front (**Figure 35**), over, and around the back (**Figure 36**). Keep the other four wires straight and close together. When you have two wraps showing on the front of the bracelet, cut the wrap wires **only** on the back of the bracelet. File the ends and press firmly into place with the pliers. **Figure 37** shows the wires before cutting. **Figure 38** shows how the front of the bracelet should look when finished.

To finish the catch end of the bracelet, take the innermost loop and bring it to the left (**Figure 39**). Wrap this loop to the back of the bracelet and press it down (**Figure 40**). **Figure 41** shows the innermost loop on the back of the bracelet. Don't flatten it completely, just snug it against the other wires. We want to keep nice, flowing curves and avoid sharp angles.

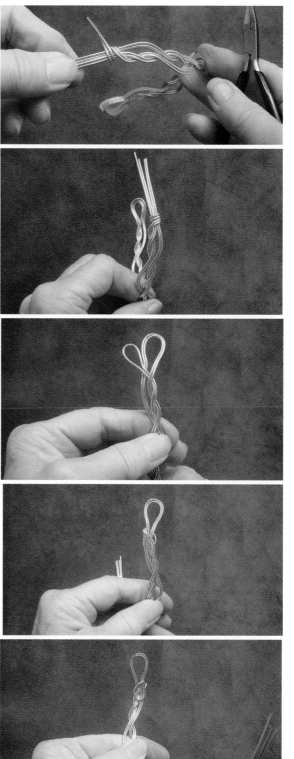

Figure 37

The back of the bracelet before cutting off the wires.

Figure 38

The front of the bracelet, showing the two wraps.

Figure 39

Pull the innermost loop to the left.

Figure 40

The innermost loop pressed firmly to the back of the bracelet.

Figure 41

The back of bracelet showing innermost loop pressed into place.

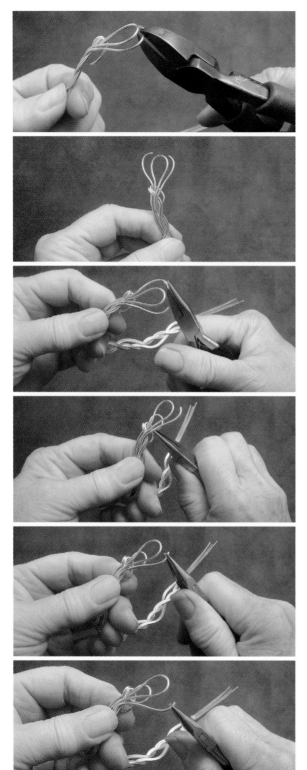

Figure 42
Cut the outermost wire.

Figure 43
The outermost loop cut in half.

Figure 44
Hold the very end of the wire with the pliers.

Figure 45
Tuck in the left wire.

Figure 46
Tuck in the right wire.

Figure 47
Adjusting the wires for the most attractive appearance.

Now cut the outermost loop somewhere near the middle. This does not have to be exact (**Figures 42 and 43**). Grasp the ends of the cut wires with needle-nose pliers and bend them to the back of the bracelet in wide, graceful curves (**Figure 44**). To avoid marring, grasp only the very ends of the cut wires with pliers or wrap the jaws of the pliers with tape.

Tuck the left and right wires into the wrap where they will not come out and irritate the skin (**Figures 45 and 46**).

After the wires are curved to the back of the bracelet, play with the placement and position them so that the front of the bracelet pleases you (**Figure 47**). Use your imagination here. Every bracelet seems to turn out differently, which is half the fun.

The remaining loop will be the catch (Figure 48). Widen the catch by placing needle-nose pliers inside the loop and pressing them open (Figure 49). Figure 50 shows the widened catch.

Just to prove nothing is written in stone, look at the circled loop in Figure 51. We decided to untuck that loop, bring it around to the front, and do a curl around the two right wires of the catch. Figure 52 shows the back of the bracelet with the new wraps on the left. This finishes the catch.

Now go back to the other end of the bracelet to finish the clasp. Be careful—there is only one chance to get this right.

Keeping the wires straight and close together (Figure 53), cut the wires about ⅝" (1.5 cm) long. File the cut ends. File lightly and toward the center from each side. Be careful, or the wires will move out of place and it will be difficult to get them back where they belong.

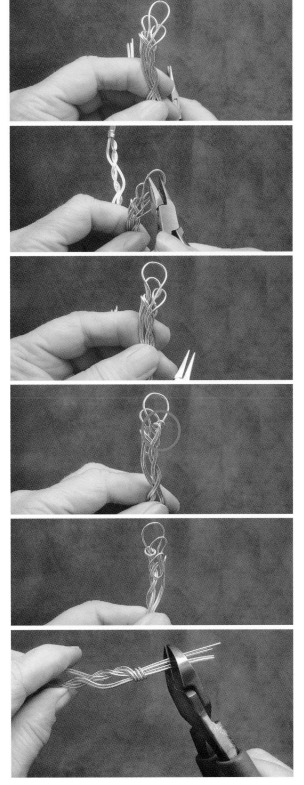

Figure 48
Wires tucked in. One remaining loop.

Figure 49
Widening the catch with needle-nose pliers.

Figure 50
The widened catch.

Figure 51
Be creative! This is the front side of the bracelet.

Figure 52
The back side of the bracelet with the new wrap on the left.

Figure 53
Cutting the wires.

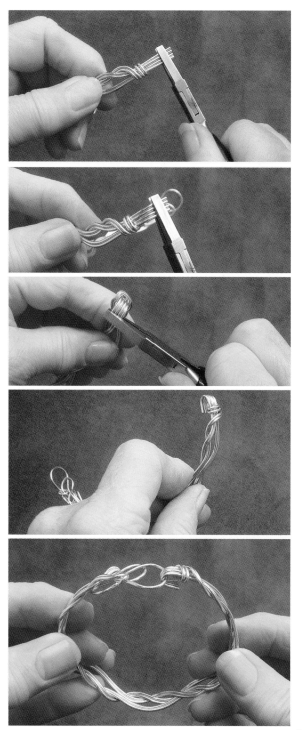

Figure 54

Place the pliers about halfway between the wrap and the cut ends.

Figure 55

Bend the wires slowly.

Figure 56

Bend a little on the right and a little on the left.

Figure 57

The finished clasp.

Figure 58

Bracelet formed into a smooth oval, catch and clasp joined.

Place either flat-nose or chain-nose pliers about halfway between the wrap and the cut ends and bend the four wires into a hook-shaped clasp (**Figure 54**). *Work slowly.* If you bend the wires down from just one side, the clasp will be crooked. Bend the wires down from the left side a little (**Figure 55**), then reposition the pliers on the right side and bend down a little more (**Figure 56**). Work back and forth until the wires form an even clasp (**Figure 57**).

Pull and form the bracelet until it is a smooth, oval shape. **Figure 58** shows the completed bracelet. For a nice finish, put the bracelet in the tumbler for several hours or overnight.

ANATOMY OF THE FREE-FORM BRACELET

Starting at the catch end of the bracelet, **Figure 59** shows the seven sections and how they alternate overlapping and underlapping. We have flattened the bracelet for demonstration purposes only. Don't do this yourself—you'd never get the bracelet to look normal again.

There are so many things that can be done with this free-form technique. Play with the many possibilities and have fun!

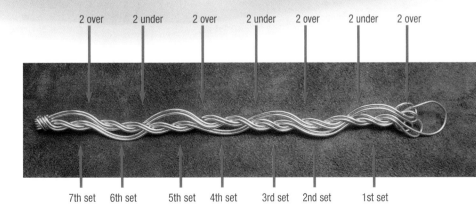

2 over   2 under   2 over   2 under   2 over   2 under   2 over

7th set   6th set   5th set   4th set   3rd set   2nd set   1st set

Figure 59

The sets and how they over- and under-lap.

woven neckpiece

All things are difficult before they are easy.
—Thomas Fuller (1654–1734)

This neckpiece is just wonderful. There is no clasp to bother with—just snap it around your neck. Everyone will appreciate its sparkling beauty and adaptability. The photograph, left, shows the neckpiece with a removable slide pendant. In Chapter 9, we'll make such a pendant.

Materials	Tools
22-gauge (0.6 mm) dead-soft round sterling silver wire	Masking tape
Flux	Needle-nose pliers
Easy sheet solder	Flat-nose pliers
	Wire cutters
	Nylon-jaw pliers
	Clamp
	Torch for soldering
	Flat file

The weaving technique is the same as that used for the woven bracelets, but with longer wires. We suggest you make the bracelet in Chapter 4 before attempting this project.

You'll be working with long wires, so pay special attention to keeping them straight and even. Work close to the clamp and only stroke the first three inches of the wires to avoid over-hardening them. Gently straighten any tangled wires.

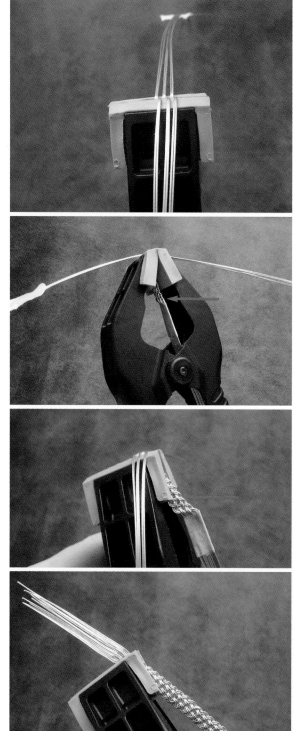

Figure 1
Beginning: three sets toward the front, three toward the back.

Figure 2
Left side after several rows have been woven. Right side of neckpiece feeds through center of clamp.

Figure 3
After weaving about 10 rows, reposition woven part to the outside of the clamp.

Figure 4
Seven inches (18 cm) woven.

The middle ¼" (6 mm) of the neckpiece remains unwoven—you'll weave outward from the center, starting with the left side.

Cut 12 wires 22" (56 cm) long. Tape one end. Wrap another piece of tape around the middle, exactly 11" (28 cm) from the taped end. This will leave 11" (28 cm) free for weaving the left side.

Open the clamp and feed the taped end through the inside of the clamp. Close the clamp jaws at the upper edge of the middle tape. This is where your weaving will start.

Separate the wires into six sets of two wires. Bend the first set toward you, the second set back, and so forth, until you have three sets at the back of the clamp and three sets at the front (**Figure 1**). Weave as described for bracelets, keeping the sets tight and close together. **Figure 2** shows the left side of the neckpiece after several rows have been woven.

Because the weave moves on a diagonal course, you will only be able to weave about ten rows before having to reposition the weaving to the outside of the clamp (**Figure 3**).

Continue to weave until you have 7" (18 cm) woven (**Figure 4**). Straighten the unwoven wires before removing the clamp (**Figure 5**). This completes the left side of the neckpiece.

Remove the piece from the clamp and remove the tape from the middle (**Figure 6**). Measure ¼" (6 mm) from the woven part and mark the unwoven wires at this point (**Figure 7**). You will leave this ¼" (6 mm) of wire unwoven before you begin weaving the right side of the neckpiece.

Move the clamp to the ¼" (6 mm) mark (**Figure 8**) and weave another 7" (18 cm). Do not take the weave out of the clamp to check your progress until you've woven at least four or five rows—the un-woven spot makes things a little unstable for a few rows (**Figure 9**).

Be sure to resume weaving with the front of the weaving facing you. If you weave with the back of the neckpiece facing you, the wire will start to curve the wrong way.

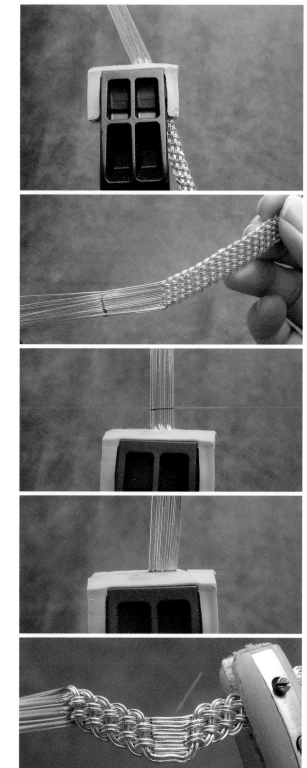

Figure 5
Straighten the un-woven wires before removing the clamp.

Figure 6
Left side completed and tape removed from middle.

Figure 7
Mark ¼" (6 mm) from woven part.

Figure 8
Move clamp to the ¼" (6 mm) mark.

Figure 9
The ¼" (6 mm) gap.

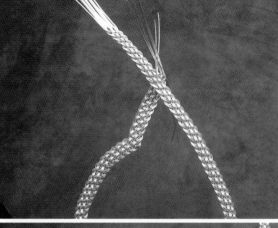

Figure 10
Things seem to have taken a turn for the worse!

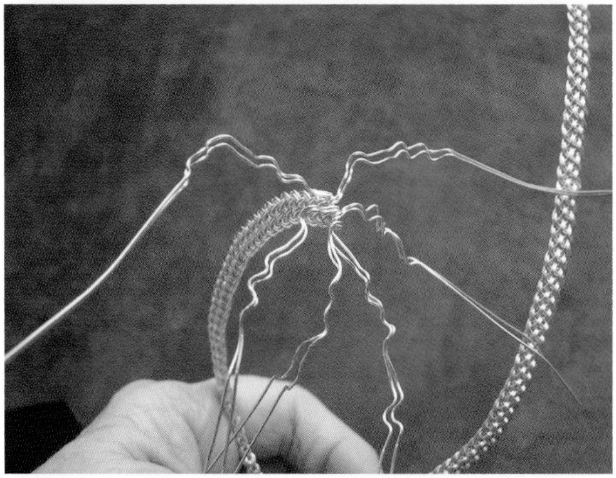

Figure 11
Mistake unwoven and looking a bit frazzled.

Figure 12
Wires after straightening with nylon pliers.

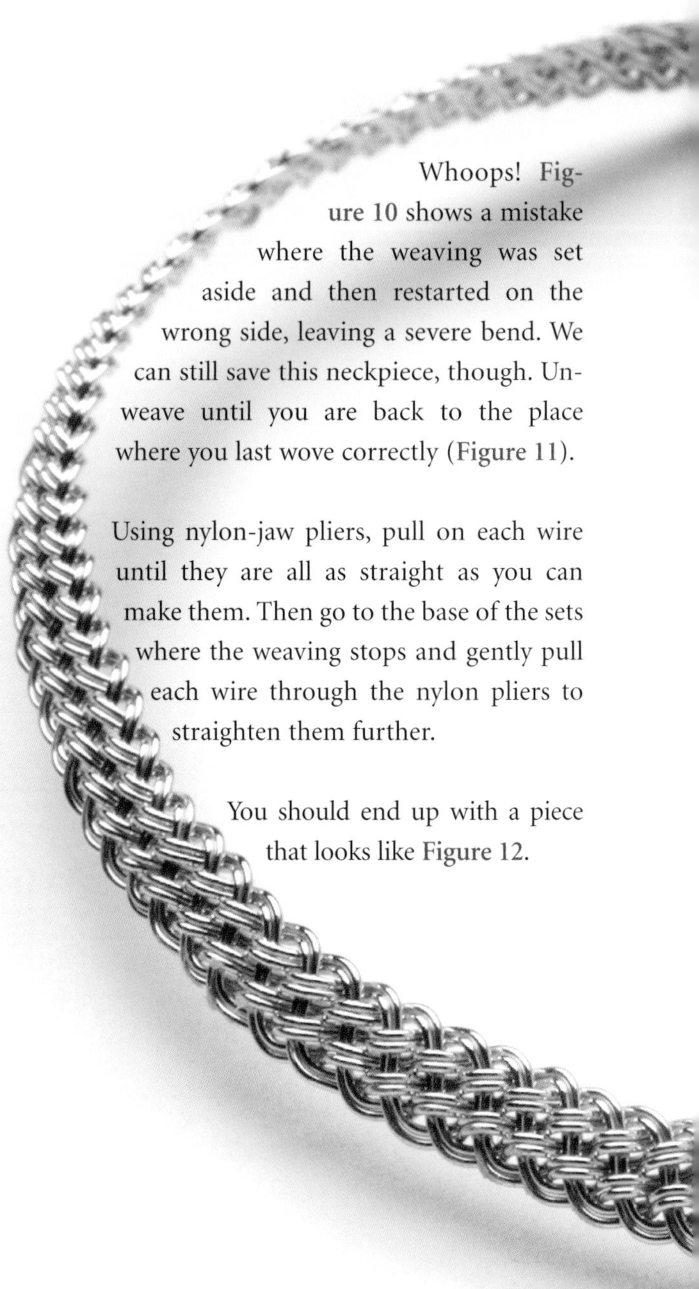

Whoops! Figure 10 shows a mistake where the weaving was set aside and then restarted on the wrong side, leaving a severe bend. We can still save this neckpiece, though. Unweave until you are back to the place where you last wove correctly (Figure 11).

Using nylon-jaw pliers, pull on each wire until they are all as straight as you can make them. Then go to the base of the sets where the weaving stops and gently pull each wire through the nylon pliers to straighten them further.

You should end up with a piece that looks like Figure 12.

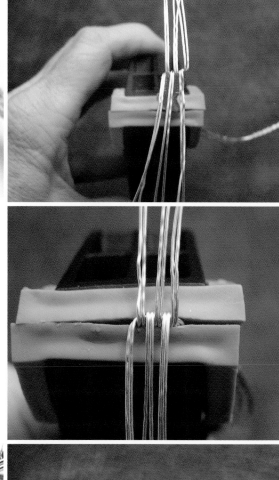

Figure 13 and Figure 14 show that the wires are just about normal again. Now weave until you have 7" (18 cm) woven on the right side to complete the neckpiece.

Figure 15 shows the finished weaving.

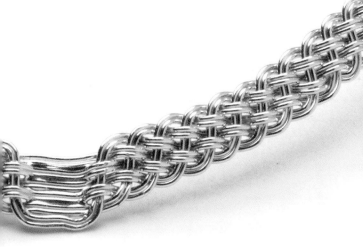

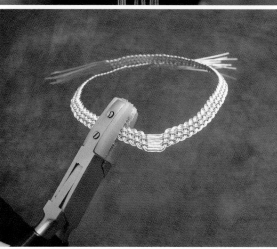

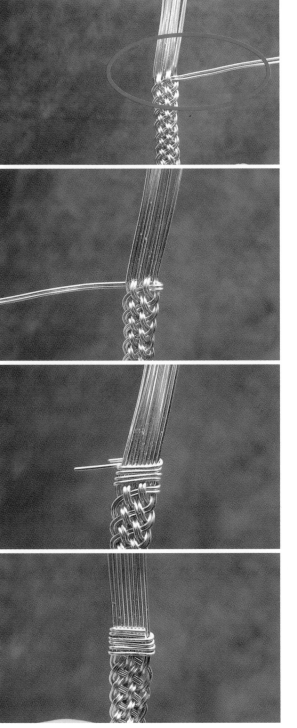

Pick up one end and find the set that has been woven over, but not brought up. Wrap this set (see circle in **Figure 16**) tightly around the other sets twice.

Figure 17 shows the set wrapped to the back.

Figure 18 shows the two completed wraps. Trim the wrapped wires on the back of the neckpiece, file them smooth, and then press firmly into place with pliers.

Figure 19 shows how the wraps should look on the back of the neckpiece. The other sets are tight, straight, and close together.

Use pliers to fold the remaining five sets to the back of the neckpiece. Fold them all at the same time, keeping them even and close together (Figure 20).

Cut the extra wire length about ⅛" (3 mm) to ¼" (6 mm) long, or enough to cover the wrapping (Figures 21 and 22). File the cut ends until smooth. File toward the center, without disturbing the wires.

Repeat steps shown by Figures 16 through Figure 22 on the opposite end of the neckpiece.

Cut the easy solder into pieces about the size of the head of a pin. Place flux and some of the solder pieces between the wraps and wires (see arrow on Figure 23).

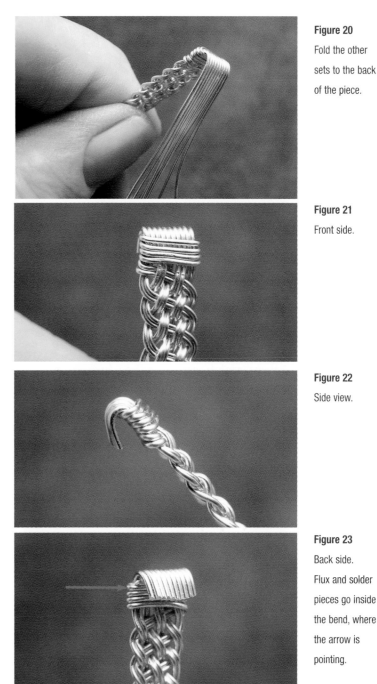

Figure 20
Fold the other sets to the back of the piece.

Figure 21
Front side.

Figure 22
Side view.

Figure 23
Back side. Flux and solder pieces go inside the bend, where the arrow is pointing.

Figure 24
Ends covered
with solder and
flux, ready to
be soldered.

Figure 25
Front side—
ends soldered.

Figure 26
Back side—
ends soldered.

Pull the wires farther down until they cover the wraps on the back of the neckpiece. Place more flux and solder pieces on top of the folded wires. Repeat on the other end (**Figure 24**).

Surround one end of the neckpiece with charcoal block, leaving ½" (1.3 cm) exposed above the charcoal. This allows you to avoid having to heat up the entire neckpiece. If the flux is not completely dry, hold the torch at a distance to dry it.

Using the very end of the flame, which is not as hot as the pointed part, heat the exposed end until the metal begins to turn red. Keep the flame constantly moving. Just as the metal begins to redden, bring the flame closer. The solder should flow at this point. Repeat the process on the other end (**Figure 25** and **Figure 26**).

Place flux and solder on the back of the unwoven wires in the middle of the neckpiece and solder as you did the ends (Figure 27). Place the neckpiece in the pickle pot until clean. Rinse the neckpiece with water to remove any remaining acid. Gently roll the neckpiece just enough to fit inside the tumbler. Avoid bending or creasing the piece. Tumble for several hours or overnight.

After tumbling, remove the piece and form it into its finished shape. Take your time, gently bending the neckpiece into a circular form. When finished, the ends of the neckpiece should overlap.

Different pendants can be slipped onto the middle of the neckpiece. See Chapter 9 for complete instructions. The flat middle of the neckpiece holds the pendant firmly, and the weaving on either side prevents the pendant from wandering off-center. Figure 28 shows the finished neckpiece with a PMC slide pendant attached.

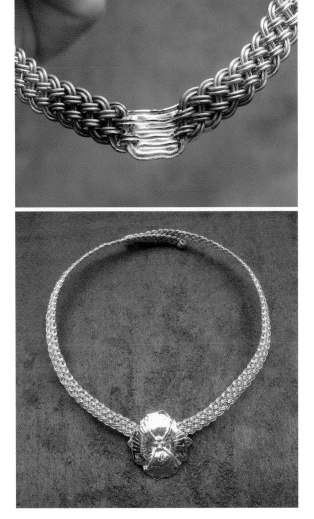

Figure 27
Back side— loose wires in the middle soldered.

Figure 28
You're finished!

Getting Creative

This neckpiece could be woven continuously without the flat portion in the center and worn without ornamentation, or, you could
❖ Add more wires to make a wider piece
❖ Use a different wire gauge

❖ Weave with gold or another metal
❖ Solder a bezel to the neckpiece to hold a stone
❖ Add a PMC piece and fire in a kiln

The possibilities are endless. Enjoy!

pendant with a woven frame

Minds are like parachutes. They only function when they are open.
—Sir James Dewar (1842–1923)

This unique pendant uses the wire-weaving technique to form a bezel. The bail opens in front and is incorporated into the pendant. The piece is a virtual playground for creativity, and we'll show you several ideas for changing its appearance. Have fun!

Materials	Tools	
Dichroic glass or stone cabochon	Clamp	Calipers
22-gauge sterling silver wire	Scribe or pencil	Easy solder
20-gauge fine silver sheet	Bezel roller	Flux
Sterling silver double half-round wire 0.204" x 0.051" (5 mm x 1.29 mm)	Flat-nose pliers	Torch
	Needle-nose pliers	Stainless steel binding wire
	Stepped/chain-nose pliers	Masking tape
	Wire cutters	Charcoal block
	Nylon-jaw pliers	Penknife
	Jeweler's saw/blade/lubricant	Bowl of cool water
	Medium solder	Dental floss

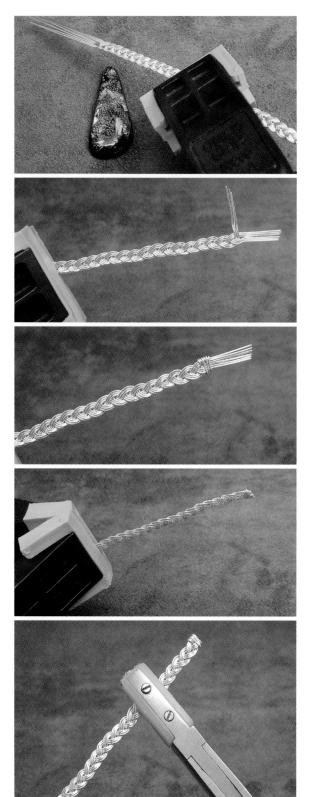

Figure 1
Dichroic glass cabochon and the woven bezel in the clamp.

Figure 2
Bend the middle set at a right angle.

Figure 3
Wrap the middle set once around the other sets.

Figure 4
Cut the remaining wires blunt to the wrap.

Figure 5
Flatten the wires with nylon-jaw pliers.

Our cabochon measures 4" (10 cm) around the perimeter. The bezel must be the same length and wide enough to bend just slightly over the front of the cabochon.

Measure the perimeter and height of your cabochon and weave the length and width of the bezel based on your measurements. Here's an easy way to make your measurements: Put masking tape around the outside edge of the cabochon, remove it, and measure the tape. Measure the height with calipers and add ⅛" (3 mm).

Cut nine wires 7" (18 cm) long and divide into three sets of three wires each. Weave (see Chapter 3 for weaving instructions) until you have a little more than 4" (10 cm) of weave. We're breaking the "even sets" rule explained in Chapter 3, but since only one side of the weave will be visible, it works in this instance.

When you have woven the desired length, remove the weaving from the clamp. Bend the middle set at a right angle and wrap this set once around the other sets. Trim the middle set on the back side of the weave. Squeeze the wires tightly into place with pliers (**Figures 2 and 3**).

Cut the remaining wires blunt to the wrap (**Figure 4**). File the ends smooth.

Flatten the entire length of the weave by squeezing it with nylon-jaw pliers (**Figure 5**).

Make a loop of masking tape with the sticky side out. Attach the cabochon to the tape to anchor it in place while you're working with the bezel (**Figure 6**).

Starting at the top, wrap the bezel around the cabochon (**Figure 7**). Keep the wire ends at the top of the cabochon so that the soldered seam eventually will be hidden by the bail. The bezel should fit tightly around the cabochon. Overlap the ends slightly and mark the unfinished bezel end at this point. The mark is where you will begin to finish this end of the bezel.

Remove the bezel from the cabochon. Bend the middle set of wires at the mark at a right angle and wrap it around the other sets as before (**Figure 8**). Cut off the remaining wires blunt to the wrap and file smooth, just as you did the other end.

Work stainless steel binding wire through the weave to hold the piece together for soldering. The woven ends should meet and fit very closely together (**Figure 9**).

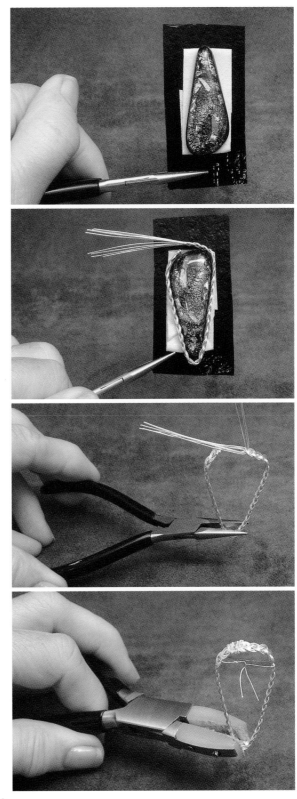

Figure 6

Anchor the cabochon with masking tape.

Figure 7

Fitting the woven bezel to the cabochon.

Figure 8

Finishing the other end of the bezel.

Figure 9

The ends should meet very closely.

Figure 10
Woven bezel on charcoal block ready to be soldered.

Figure 11
The soldered bezel after quenching.

Figure 12
Checking the bezel for fit.

Figure 13
Marking the silver sheet for soldering and sawing.

Lay the bezel on a charcoal block (Figure 10). Apply flux to the area to be soldered with a small pointed brush. The flux should have the consistency of thick cream. Add chips of medium solder around the seam where the two ends of the bezel meet. Don't worry about the binding wire during soldering. It may burn or solder onto your piece, but it will pull off easily and won't do any harm.

Solder and let the piece air-cool (Figure 11). *Remove the binding wire* and put the woven bezel in the pickle pot to clean. *Never put binding wire in the pickle.* After pickling, rinse the bezel in water.

Place the cabochon inside the bezel to check the fit (Figure 12). The woven bezel should fit the cabochon tightly and should be just high enough to bend over the top of the cabochon. If the bezel doesn't fit correctly, you'll have to make another. As carpenters say, "Measure twice and cut once."

Lay the cabochon with the bezel in place on a sheet of fine silver and trace around it with a pencil or scribe (Figure 13). Rough out a shape in the sheet metal with a jeweler's saw (Figure 14).

Remove the cabochon and paint flux on the sheet metal and the bottom of the woven bezel (**Figure 15**). Place the bezel on top of the sheet metal so that the fluxed surfaces are touching.

To hold the bezel in place, thread binding wire through the weave and wrap it around the sheet metal. Make several wraps, working your way from top to bottom (**Figures 16 and 17**).

If you were to simply put the binding wire on top of the woven bezel, the bezel might collapse. Tighten the wire as you thread it through the bezel. Tie off the wire firmly on the back of the sheet metal.

Bend the binding wire on the front of the piece with pliers to tighten it. The bezel and sheet metal should be snug, but not so tight that the bezel bends during soldering (**Figure 18**).

Place more flux and small pieces of medium solder on the sheet metal against the bezel, both inside and out. Use a damp (not wet) brush to pick up and

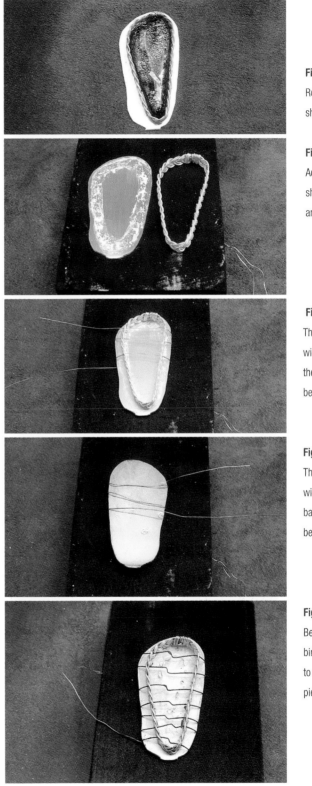

Figure 14
Rough out a shape.

Figure 15
Add flux to the sheet metal and bezel.

Figure 16
Thread binding wire through the woven bezel.

Figure 17
The binding wires on the back of the bezel.

Figure 18
Bend the binding wire to make the pieces snug.

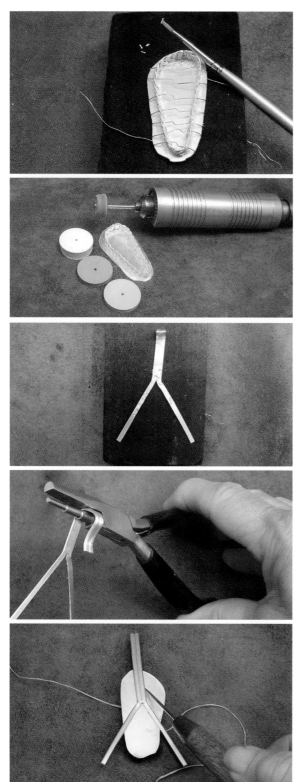

Figure 19
Place solder chips around the inside and outside of the bezel.

Figure 20
Disks for shaping the outside of the frame.

Figure 21
Saw the wire and spread the legs.

Figure 22
Shaping the bail.

Figure 23
Mark the placement of the bail.

place the solder (**Figure 19**). The solder chips will stay in place when the flux dries.

While soldering, concentrate the torch flame on the sheet metal and let it heat up first, then move the flame to the solder near the bezel. Keep the flame moving at all times. After soldering, quench the piece in cool water and clean in the pickle pot.

Use a file or a flex-shaft to give the outside of the sheet metal its final shape. **Figure 20** shows a rubber Cratex wheel on the flex-shaft. The white disk is used for cutting, the blue for smoothing, and the pink for finishing. Use whichever disk is necessary to get the effect you want, or simply saw the extra metal off and smooth it flush to finish.

MAKING THE BAIL

To make the bail, cut a piece of double half-round wire 3" (7.5 cm) long. Mark the halfway point, place the wire in the ring clamp, and saw the legs apart. (Figure 21). Spread the legs apart with a penknife and file any rough edges smooth.

Rough out the shape of the top of the bail with stepped/chain-nose pliers (**Figure 22**). We'll give the bail its final shape a little later. Place the bail on the back of the piece and, when you are pleased with its location, trace the bail outline onto the sheet metal with a scribe or pencil (**Figure 23**).

Solder, quench, remove the binding wire, and pickle the piece. Tumble for several hours to clean the inside before adding the cabochon. Hold the pieces together with binding wire. Flux the back of the sheet metal and add solder pieces along the edges of the bail. Solder, quench, and pickle the piece.

Figure 24 shows a bezel roller, also known as a bezel rocker. (Whether you choose rock or roll, this is the tool to use to press the bezel against the cabochon.)

Place the cabochon into the bezel frame and secure with a bezel roller. Use a rocking (or rolling) motion to press the bezel against and over the cabochon edges. The bezel needs to cover only a small part of the cabochon all the way around the perimeter. Press and rock the bezel roller at the twelve o'clock position, then the six o'clock, then the nine o'clock, and three o'clock. Continue around the bezel until it is pressed evenly against the cabochon (Figure 25). The woven bezel should cover the front of the cabochon just enough to hold it securely in place.

Smooth and round the ends of the legs and tip of the bail with a file or flex-shaft. Use round- or chain-nose pliers to bend the bail to the front of the piece. The bail should cover the soldered part of the bezel and a small part of the cabochon. Make a graceful curve that pleases you. Use a jeweler's saw to cut through the middle of the bail and separate the wires. You may also choose to leave the bail whole. Bend the bezel legs to the front of the pendant and position them any way that you like. Tumble the piece for four hours or overnight.

Figure 26 shows the back of the pendant.

Figure 24

A bezel roller.

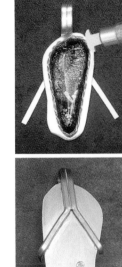

Figure 25

Press the bezel into place.

Figure 26

Back of the pendant.

The Finished Piece

You can see that we have left some silver sheet extending beyond the bezel. If we had made a pendant without the lower legs (they're only decorative), we might have added gold or silver balls or even gemstones.

Use your imagination in choosing the cabochon, making the bezel and bail, and adding ornamentation. Slip your pendant on any necklace, including the neckpiece in this book, and get ready for compliments!

precious metal clay

Imagination is the beginning of creation. You imagine what you desire, you will what you imagine and at last you create what you will.
—George Bernard Shaw (1856–1950)

For many jewelry makers, Precious Metal Clay (PMC) is the best invention since the mute button on the remote. You can make PMC jewelry with your hands and a few simple tools. PMC can be hand-formed, used in a push-mold, carved, and sanded. There is another precious metal clay on the market called Art Clay, and it can be used in place of PMC. It does have slightly different properties, though, so be sure to read the accompanying literature if you choose to use it. We use PMC because we are more familiar with it, but we are not endorsing one metal clay over another.

An Introduction to Precious Metal Clay

Photo courtesy The Bell Group/Rio Grande

PMC is pure silver or pure gold mixed with an organic binder to make a clay-like substance. When PMC is fired in a kiln, the binder burns away to leave a piece of jewelry that is pure silver or pure gold. The piece can then be treated as any other metal—it can be soldered, pickled, engraved, drilled, and hammered. It's also possible to add more PMC to a fired piece and re-fire it. This feature gives you the opportunity to correct mistakes, or to add new elements to a PMC piece.

Most people prefer to use synthetic stones in their PMC. Many natural stones cannot survive the heat produced during firing. Also, you may inadvertently "heat treat" a natural stone and change its color. The stones you use may be any shape and they may be pressed into the clay or mounted in a PMC bezel. The projects in this chapter demonstrate a few of the many things that can be done with this wonderful material.

PMC silver comes in regular, PMC+, and PMC3. At the date of this writing, gold PMC comes in regular form only. The data below will help you decide which PMC is best for your particular project.

ORIGINAL PMC

Firing Temperature: 1650°F (900°C) for two hours.

Available in clay, slip, and syringe

Shrink rate: 28%

Pros: Because it holds a high percentage of binder material, this clay dries more slowly than other PMC formulas. Slow drying makes it the easiest clay to work with because it stays workable for a longer time.

Cons: When fired, it is more porous and, as a result, somewhat more fragile than silver sheet. The high shrink-rate will produce smaller pieces, which is an important consideration.

PMC+

Firing Temperature:

1650°F (900°C) for 10 minutes

1560°F (850°C) for 20 minutes

1470°F (800°C) for 30 minutes

Available in lump, slip, paste, and paper forms. The Japanese use the paper for metal origami, which can be woven and braided.

Shrink rate: 12–15%

Pros: Comes in many forms, is denser than original PMC, which makes the fired clay less fragile and porous, and can be fired at a wider range of times and temperatures. Shrinks less than original PMC.

Cons: PMC+ is a little more expensive than original PMC.

PMC3

Firing Temperature:

1290°F (700°C) for 10 minutes

1200°F (650°C) for 20 minutes

1110°F (600°C) for 30 minutes

Available in lump form only.

Shrink rate: 12–15% (about the same as PMC+)

Pros: Fires at very low temperatures very quickly.

Cons: Has a tendency to develop cracks while drying.

Slip or paste can be made from any of the PMC products. It's advisable to use PMC+ slip with PMC+ clay so the shrink rates are compatible. Slip is made by mixing PMC with water until it is the consistency of whipping cream. Dried-out clay can be reconstituted by chopping it into tiny pieces and mixing with water. Some people use a little coffee grinder for chopping dried-out clay, and that's okay as long as the grinder is used for this purpose only.

Another recovery technique is to soak the pieces in a plastic bag with water, then knead the mixture (still in the plastic) to a smooth consistency. It's very difficult to get reconstituted clay to act exactly like clay fresh from the package, but reconstitution is better than losing the clay altogether. Be sure to mark the containers so you'll know which clay you used to make the slip.

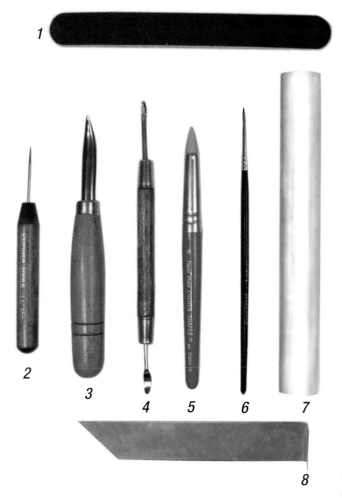

PMC TOOLS AND EQUIPMENT

1. Fingernail file. This is a broad, flexible metal nail file that has a rough side and a smoother side, and both sides can be used to sand and smooth the dried, unfired clay. These files are commonly found at grocery stores and pharmacies.

2. Pick or needle tool. We use this to add detail to soft clay and to remove excess PMC from an unfired piece. You may use a darning needle and/or long sewing needle instead, but the handle on the pick makes it comfortable and, if you should drop your tool, the handle makes a pick easier to find than a needle. You can also make a handle for a darning or sewing needle. Just roll a piece of polymer clay into a handle shape, press your needle into place on one end and bake in the oven for the time designated on the polymer clay package.

3. Burnishing tool. After firing, a PMC piece will need to be burnished at any spots where you intend to add solder. Fired PMC is more porous than regular silver due to the tiny holes that result from the burning-off of the binders in the clay. Solder simply will not adhere to this porous surface. Burnishing compresses the clay and makes it less porous so it will accept solder.

4. Kemper sculpting tool. We used a sculpting tool to shape the polymer clay blossom in this chapter. Kemper tools are very useful for sculpting both polymer and PMC clay, and they're found in ceramic supply stores and hobby shops. There are many different varieties to choose from and they are relatively inexpensive, so you'll probably want to buy several.

5. Blending tool. This tool has a very soft rubber tip for blending in cracks and for other finishing work with PMC. It's our favorite PMC tool. Any jewelry supplier that sells PMC will probably stock the blending tool. See Resources in the back of this book for more information.

6. Paintbrush. Paintbrushes are used to blend cracks, re-wet dried areas, and for applying slip.

7. PVC pipe, ½" diameter. We use this pipe to roll out PMC into strips. Will a regular rolling pin work? Of course! Anything round will do the job—but keep PMC rolling pins separate from rolling pins used in your kitchen.

8. L-shaped or tissue knife. Made of stainless steel, this knife is used to cut PMC into shapes. It also comes in handy for lifting soft PMC off your work surface.

A Formica surface, a plastic placemat, or an untextured plastic cutting board all make good work surfaces. If there is new home construction near you, ask the workers for the sink cutout. It will usually be a good piece of Formica perfect for your work surface.

Craft sticks or tongue depressors can be used to roll PMC out into thin, even slabs or strips.

Craft foam is available at hobby stores and is used as a very gentle "sandpaper" for cleaning up the edges of PMC.

Olive oil is applied sparingly to the work surface and to your hands to keep the PMC from sticking.

A bowl of water should always be nearby so that you can dampen your paintbrush.

PMC is usually placed on a kiln shelf during firing. Round and delicate pieces, however, are often fired in a terra-cotta dish on a bed of either alumina hydrate (also known as kiln wash) or vermiculite. Such a bed prevents the PMC pieces from rolling around and provides a good surface for complicated pieces that might deform on a smooth, hard surface. Alumina hydrate can be found at most places that sell PMC, or at a ceramics store. You can pick up vermiculite at any garden center while you're buying your terra-cotta dishes.

When you begin a PMC project, gather all your tools and put them close to your work surface. You don't want to stop in the middle of a project and hunt for a tool—PMC dries much too quickly.

PMC should be fired in a computer-controlled kiln, which allows the clay to stay at the same temperature for a designated length of time. PMC suppliers sell a dedicated PMC kiln. If your budget allows, purchase a kiln that will also fire enamels and glass. Ceramics kilns are sometimes used for PMC, but the results are usually unsatisfactory because ceramic kilns tend to have hot and cold spots. Ceramics have a higher tolerance for temperature variations than PMC, which requires precise temperature control.

It is possible to fire small PMC pieces with a torch. Ideally, you would use a microtorch such as the Blazer torch for this purpose. Blazer torches can be found at gourmet shops where they are sold for carmelizing sugar for crême brulée. Torch-firing PMC, however, is still experimental and, as of this date, the results are not dependable.

Other items that you will need for PMC work are inexpensive and are probably already in your home.

domed bracelet with pmc bead ends

What we learn to do, we learn by doing.
—Aristotle (384–322 B.C.)

This is the same bracelet as on page 42, but with no soldering. We're going to use PMC slip to "glue" the beads onto the ends of the bracelet. Gluing is much easier than soldering.

Materials	**Tools**
22-gauge (0.5 mm) round dead-soft sterling silver wire	PMC tools
PMC3 slip	Kiln
PMC3 clay	Jeweler's saw
Two 12 to 15 mm Bali beads (or any sterling silver bead of your choice)	Saw lubricant
	Wire cutters
	Flat-nose pliers
	Nylon-jaw pliers
	Rubber mallet
	Rawhide mallet
	Clamp
	Ring clamp
	Paintbrush
	Olive oil

Figure 1
Woven piece domed. The ends have been folded under to fit the bead.

Figure 2
Saw off part of the bead.

Figure 3
Bead cut off and ready to check for fit.

Figure 4
A good fit.

Figure 5
Coat the end with PMC3 slip.

Each wire will be a set. This is a single-weave bracelet. Cut thirty-six wires 10½" (26.5 cm) long. Weave a piece 6½" (16.5 cm) long. (See Chapter 3 for weaving techniques and Chapter 5 for specific bracelet instructions.) Cut off the taped end and any extra length from the opposite end. Dome the woven piece and bend the ends to narrow them to fit the bead (**Figure 1**).

Choose two sterling silver beads and place one in a ring clamp. Saw off ¼ to ⅓ of the bead as you did in Chapter 5 (**Figure 2**).

Figure 3 shows the bead cut off and ready to check for fit on the bracelet end. If the bead is too large or too small, make any necessary adjustments (see Chapter 5).

Do not to use binding wire with PMC. Binding wire will stick to the clay and can cause discoloration.

Figure 4 shows that the bead fits well on the woven end. Repeat the process with the second bead on the opposite end of the weave.

Coat one end of the bracelet and the inside of the bead with PMC3 slip (**Figure 5**).

Rub your hands lightly with olive oil, then take a small amount of PMC3 clay, roll it into a ball, and press it inside the bead (**Figure 6**). Place just enough clay inside the bead to hold it firmly to the wire, while at the same time leaving enough room to insert the woven end. You want to avoid having clay squeeze out onto the woven end.

If you do get clay on the woven end (**Figure 7**), dampen a paintbrush—just damp, not wet—and use it to remove the excess clay. After the clay is dry, apply the damp brush again to remove any residual material.

Using the same steps as above, attach a bead to the opposite end of the bracelet. Allow the bracelet to dry thoroughly. **Figure 8** shows how the bracelet should look at this point.

After the clay is completely dry, place the bracelet in the kiln and fire at 1110°F (600°C) for 30 minutes.

Figure 9 shows one of those little surprises that sometimes occur in jewelry making. In this case, the bracelet blackened in the kiln. Our theory is that the antique finish on the bead spread over the bracelet while it was being fired. Perhaps this is where the old saying, "We've got ourselves in a real pickle," came from, because that's exactly what we had to do—put the bracelet in the pickle pot to clean it. **Figure 10** shows the bracelet right after pickling.

Make your bracelet sparkle by putting it into the tumbler for several hours, or overnight.

For a more finished look, we added a wrap made out of 14-gauge (1.6 mm) half-round sterling silver wire below each bead. (See Chapters 3 and 4 for wrapping instructions.) You can also make a wrap out of PMC3 strips, and fire the bracelet again. Let the bracelet cool before pickling or rinsing. **Figure 11** shows the finished bracelet.

Figure 6
PMC3 pressed inside the bead.

Figure 7
Remove excess PMC from the weave with a damp paintbrush.

Figure 8
Front of bracelet before firing.

Figure 9
This isn't as bad as it looks!

Figure 10
The bracelet after pickling.

Figure 11
The finished bracelet.

woven cuff bracelet
with pmc beads

> *Idea and execution are not often*
> *entrusted to the same head.*
> –Ralph Waldo Emerson (1803–1882)

Here's another domed cuff with a weave that uses sets of three wires instead of two. Use PMC3 to form beads that attach to the woven ends. We've added PMC3 bezels with synthetic sapphire cabochons for a luxurious look.

Materials	Tools
22-gauge (0.5 mm) round dead-soft sterling silver wire	PMC tools
2 synthetic sapphire cabochons (4 mm)	Olive oil
1 package of PMC3 (about 25 grams)	Paintbrush
PMC3 clay	Ruler
	Plastic wrap to keep PMC moist
	600 grit sandpaper
	Aluminum foil
	Tweezers
	PMC kiln
	Tumbler

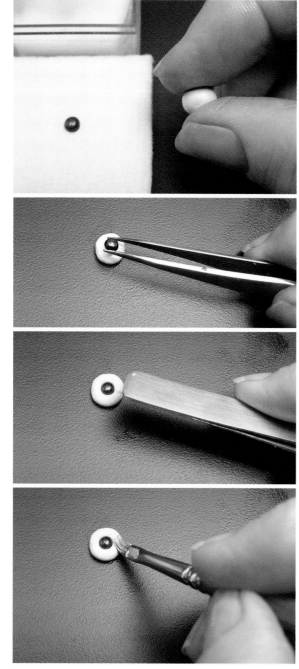

Figure 1
Roll out a pea-sized piece of clay.

Figure 2
Flatten the clay and place a bead in the middle.

Figure 3
Press the bead into the clay.

Figure 4
Smooth out any cracks with a damp brush.

Refer to pages 14–21 for weaving technique and to pages 44–48 for specific bracelet instructions. Cut 30 sterling silver wires 10½" (26.5 cm) long. Tape one end, place in the clamp, and divide the wires into sets of three. Weave until you have a piece 6½" (16.5 cm) long. Cut off the taped end and any extra wire from the other end. Taper the ends as shown in Chapter 5.

Do not use binding wire with PMC. Binding wire will stick to the clay and can cause discoloration.

Make sure to have all your PMC tools and materials ready before you start. Put olive oil on your work surface and on your hands. Formica makes a great work surface, or you can use a plastic placemat or heavy plastic.

Pinch off a pea-sized piece of PMC3 and roll it into a ball (**Figure 1**). Flatten the ball and use tweezers to pick up a cabochon and place it in the middle of the clay (**Figure 2**). Press the cabochon into the clay until the bead is slightly below the top surface of the clay (**Figure 3**).

Wet a paintbrush, blot it on a paper towel to remove excess water, and smooth any cracks in the clay. You may have to let the piece dry and repeat this process several times to smooth out all the cracks. (**Figure 4**).

After the clay bezel is thoroughly dry and has no cracks (this could take a while!), use either an emery board or 600-grit sandpaper to further smooth and refine the bezel.

Repeat the process with the other cabochon and let both bezels dry completely. Pinch off enough PMC3 to make two ends for the bracelet. To ensure that both ends are the same size, roll out the PMC3 evenly, measure with a ruler, and cut or pinch off at the midway point.

Make sure that your hands and work surface are lightly coated with olive oil. Roll each piece of PMC3 into a ball and press onto the ends of the woven piece (**Figure 5**). Wrap one end in plastic so it doesn't dry out while you're working on the other end.

Mold the clay into a round shape (**Figure 6**). Be sure to pay equal attention to the back side of the piece. **Figure 7** shows the back of the bracelet.

Use a damp paintbrush to smooth out any cracks. Let the clay dry and repeat the smoothing as necessary (**Figure 8**). Repeat the process on the other end of the bracelet. Let the ends dry completely and use sandpaper to refine the shape and further smooth the clay.

To add the small clay bezel, paint PMC3 slip on the PMC3 end where you wish to place the bezel (**Figure 9**). The slip will act as glue to hold the two pieces together. Repeat on the other end, then set the bracelet in crumpled foil to stabilize it while finishing.

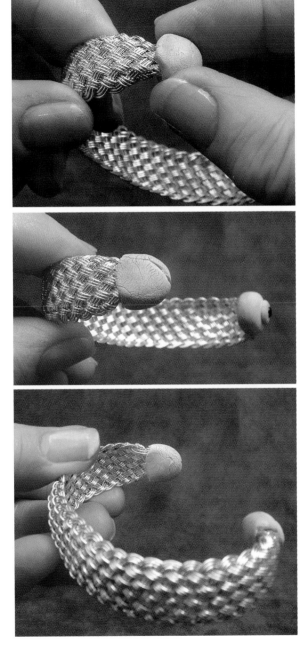

Figure 5
Press the ball onto the end of the woven piece.

Figure 6
Form the PMC3 ball into shape.

Figure 7
The back of the bracelet.

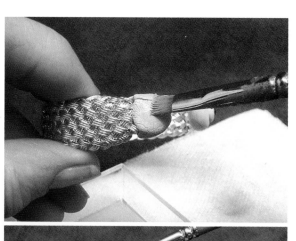

Figure 8
Smooth out any cracks with a damp brush.

Figure 9
Add slip where the bezel will be placed.

Figure 10
Place the bezel on the PMC3 end.

Use tweezers to place the bezels on the PMC3 ends (**Figure 10**). Brush a little more slip around the bezels and the PMC3 ends to further bond the pieces.

When the piece is dry, use a darning needle and 600-grit sandpaper or an emery board to clean and refine the area around the stones. Doing so will give the bezels nice beveled edges (**Figure 11**).

Figure 12 shows the finished bracelet ready to fire. Fire at 1110°F (600°C) for 30 minutes.

Figure 13 shows the bracelet after firing. Although the cracks are hard to see, a few remain in the fired PMC3, caused by shrinkage around the wires. The cracks are easy to fix. Fill them with more PMC3, let the piece dry, and sand to smooth. Refire the bracelet at the same temperature for the same length of time as before.

Put the bracelet in the tumbler for several hours or overnight. Wear and enjoy, or give it to a friend!

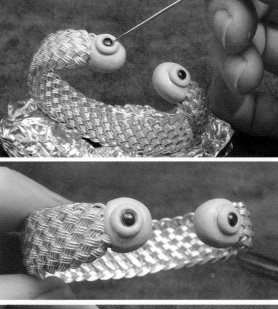

Figure 11
Clean and bevel the stone mounting.

Figure 12
Ready to fire.

Figure 13
Out of the kiln, with a few little cracks to fill.

Figure 14
The finished bracelet after tumbling.

precious metal clay bracelet

This bracelet is an excellent example of the wonderful things you can create from Precious Metal Clay. After firing in the kiln, the bracelet is transformed into pure silver. It is very light after firing, yet sturdy. The texture on this bracelet comes from a cut crystal glass. You can use rubber stamps, grasses and plants, lace, pasta (uncooked, please) or anything else that makes a pattern that pleases you. With PMC, you are only limited by your imagination. Something this pretty shouldn't be so easy to make!

Materials

Original PMC (two packages or 60 g)

A variety of synthetic gemstones measuring 4 mm or less

Toggle clasp

Half-hard, half-round 14-gauge (1.63 mm) sterling silver wire (for the bracelet links)

28-gauge (0.321 mm) fine silver round wire

22-gauge (0.644 mm) fine silver round wire

22-gauge (0.644 mm) 24k gold round wire

Tools

PMC tools

Olive oil

Emery board or nail file

400- or 320-grit sandpaper

Drinking straws (various diameters cut into thirds)

Craft sticks or tongue depressors

Plastic wrap

Formica work surface

Paintbrush

Fine round file

Stepped/chain-nose pliers

Bowl of water

Wire mesh

Tweezers

Kiln

Plastic bags to keep clay moist

4 jump rings, 9.5 mm, 16-gauge

Figure 1
Embellishments.

Figure 2
Bend the ends of the woven pieces at a 90° angle.

Figure 3
Pre-set stones.

Figure 4
Roll the clay into a ball and flatten on your work surface.

Make the embellishments for the bracelet first. The woven piece at the top of **Figure 1** is made of 28-gauge (0.321 mm) fine silver woven in four sets of two wires. The piece beneath is of the same gauge, but it's woven as twelve sets of one wire. Make each weave 4" to 6" (10 cm to 15 cm) long. The width will be about ¼" (6 mm).

The star-shaped piece in **Figure 1** is 24k, 22-gauge (0.644 mm) gold round wire that has been crimped with pliers. The curlicues are of the same wire twisted randomly. The tiny gold balls with the stems are also made of the same wire. The silver ball is made of 22-gauge (0.321 mm) fine silver wire.

Make the little balls by cutting round wire into ¼" (6 mm) lengths. Heat up one end of the wire with a torch until it forms a ball. Leave the other end straight to use as a stem. These stems will be pushed into the PMC to help hold the balls in place.

Using pliers and/or your fingers, bend and curve portions of the woven pieces, then cut them into segments of varying lengths, about ¼" to ½" (6 mm to 1.3 cm). Create sizes and shapes that please you.

Use flat-nose pliers to bend one row of weaving at a 90° angle on both ends of each woven piece (**Figure 2**). These bent ends will be pressed into the PMC clay to hold the woven pieces in place. Reserve a few woven pieces to wrap around some of the preset stones (**Figure 3**).

Now we'll make those preset stones in **Figure 3**. Have all your PMC supplies close at hand. PMC dries very quickly—if you are going to leave your work, even for a moment, cover the clay with plastic wrap. First, we'll make settings out of PMC and then set the synthetic stones in them.

Lightly coat your work surface and your hands with olive oil. Unwrap the PMC and pinch off a piece the size of a pea. Roll the piece into a smooth ball (**Figure 4**) and flatten it on the work surface.

Use a drinking straw slightly smaller than the stone to press a hole through the middle of the clay. Press the straw all the way through, rotate it to release it from the clay, and remove the straw and the "donut" hole (**Figures 5 and 6**). Smooth out any cracks in the clay with your oiled finger or a damp paintbrush.

Pick up a stone with tweezers and place it in the hole (**Figure 7**). Press the stone into the hole so its top lies slightly beneath the surface of the clay. Put the piece on a scrap of wire mesh or anything that will allow the air to circulate freely on all sides of the piece. Doing so will help the clay to dry evenly.

Figures 8 and 9 show the front and back of the stones set in PMC. We've left the back of the setting open. We're using a faceted stone, and the opening allows light to pass through, giving it extra sparkle. You may also opt to cover the back of the stone with clay to enhance the color of the stone.

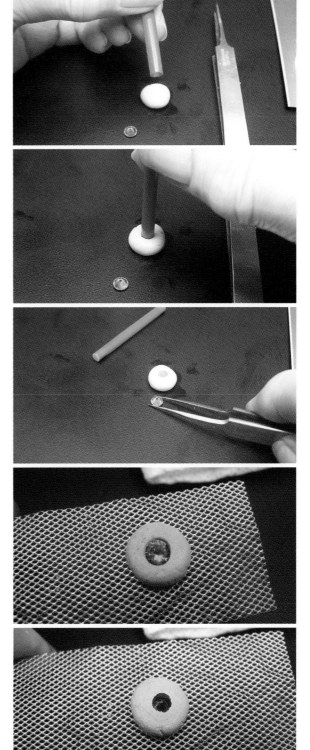

Figure 5

Choose a straw with a diameter slightly larger than your stone.

Figure 6

Press the straw through the middle of the clay.

Figure 7

The center clay is removed. Ready to place the stone.

Figure 8

Front of the set stone.

Figure 9

Back of the set stone.

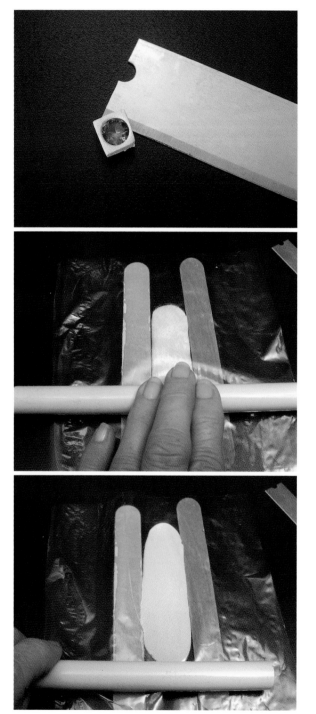

Figure 10
Bezel made smaller.

Figure 11
Craft sticks and clay ready to roll out.

Figure 12
Clay rolled flat.

Try lots of different sizes and shapes for settings, as in **Figure 3**. **Figure 10** shows a set stone that has had the bezel cut down with a tissue knife while still wet. The bezel can be left as in **Figure 10** or you can cut the corners off with a tissue knife. After drying, this bezel can be sanded until it is a thin band surrounding the stone.

To wrap a setting in a woven piece, roll the weave around a dowel or pencil to form a tight circle. Open up the circle and place the setting carefully inside. The ends of the woven piece should evenly abut.

Now we'll make the sections for the bracelet. *It is important that the stone settings be completely dry before you begin this part of the bracelet.*

Lightly coat your work surface and hands with olive oil. Roll the remaining PMC into a long snake and flatten it into a rectangle. Place a craft stick on either side of the clay and cover the arrangement with a plastic bag (**Figure 12**).

Use a ½" (1.3 cm) diameter PVC pipe (or whatever you have chosen as a rolling pin) to roll the clay flat and even (**Figure 13**). Roll the clay until it is the same thickness as the craft sticks.

Remove the plastic covering and use the craft sticks to square up the sides and ends of the clay (**Figures 14 and 15**).

We've used a piece of cut glass to give this piece an interesting pattern (**Figure 16**). Use whatever you like for texture and press it evenly into the clay (**Figure 17**).

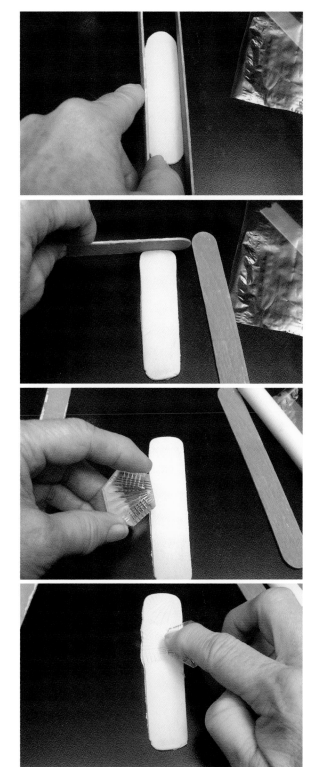

Figure 14
Use the craft sticks to square the sides of the clay.

Figure 15
Square the ends.

Figure 16
Cut glass for creating a pattern in the clay.

Figure 17
Press the pattern into the clay.

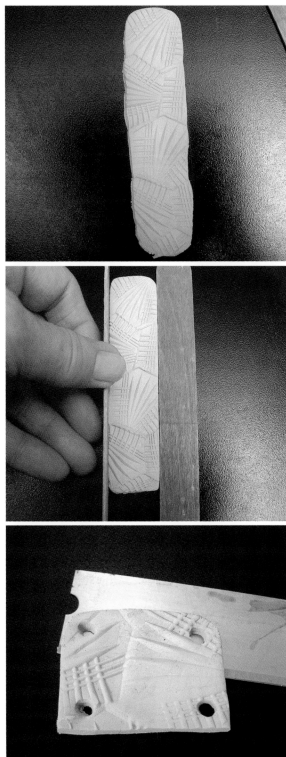

Figure 18
Pattern pressed into the clay.

Figure 19
Reshape the clay to its original width and thickness.

Figure 20
Corner holes punched for the connecting links.

Pressing will thin and widen the clay (**Figure 18**). When you are happy with the look, use the craft sticks to push the clay back to its original thickness and 1" (2.5 cm) width (**Figure 19**).

We have decided to make each section square. Use a tissue knife to cut the sections 1" (2.5 cm) long. You can calculate the length of the bracelet easily in this example because the sections are 1" (2.5 cm) long. We'll cut six sections for this bracelet, which should give us a finished length of about 6½" (16.5 cm). Change the length and number of sections to fit the wearer's wrist size.

Pick the sections up with the tissue knife to separate them from each other. With a narrow drinking straw, punch corner holes through the clay for the connecting links (**Figure 20**).

Use a large-diameter drinking straw to punch holes for the preset gems in whatever pattern you like (**Figure 21**). Push the straw all the way through and rotate it as before. Any clay that doesn't lift out with the straw can be removed with tweezers. Save clay scraps to make slip.

If the clay has begun to dry, making the holes may cause the edge of the section to bulge slightly. Resquare the section with craft sticks.

Paint PMC slip on the backs of the preset stones and press them gently into place over their holes (Figure 22). Remember to wrap the sections you are not working on in plastic to keep them from drying out.

Figure 21
Additional holes punched for the preset gems.

Figure 22
Preset gems over the holes.

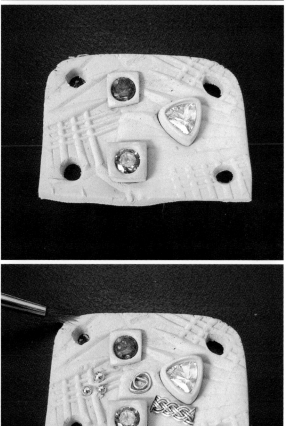

Figure 23 shows a finished section. The preset stones have been pressed into place, and we've added a piece of woven wire, three gold balls, and a gold curlicue. Press the ends of the woven wire into the clay.

Figure 23
Embellishments in place.

Figure 24
Drying the
sections.

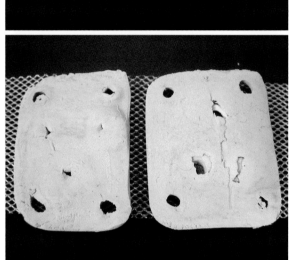

Figure 25
The section
backs.

Figure 26
The stones
have fallen out.

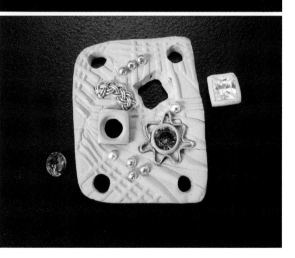

Pressing embellishments into place deforms the section. If the section is still very pliable, you can restore the square shape with the craft sticks. You can resquare a dried-out section by sanding its edges lightly. Use a damp paintbrush to smooth any places that have dried out or cracked.

Because we have added so many embellishments, the shrinkage will somewhat deform the sections when the clay is fired. Don't worry if this happens—you'll find that your sections look more interesting than if they were perfectly square.

Place the finished sections on a piece of wire mesh (avoid aluminum), as you did with the bezels, and let them dry completely (Figure 24). Drying can take as long as twenty-four hours. After the sections are dry, use an emery board or nail file to clean up the edges and round the corners. Pay equal attention to the backs of the sections. Use a round file to smooth out any rough spots in the linking holes.

Figure 25 shows the backs of two sections. Smooth out cracks or rough areas with a damp paintbrush. If needed, use PMC slip to fill in cracks and sand smooth. Use a small round file to make the connecting holes round and even. Sand the section backs flat. If necessary, open up any holes that may have closed or that have slip on them so that your gems will have a chance to sparkle.

TROUBLESHOOTING

Figure 26 shows that two stones have fallen out after drying. To reattach the purple stone on the left, make the bezel slightly wider with a file, dampen the hole with a wet paintbrush, and replace the stone. The stone should be seated a little deeper now.

To replace the preset stone on the right, paint a little PMC slip around the hole and press the stone back into place.

Figure 27 shows a gold curlicue that needs to be reattached. Use any pointed object to deepen the depression on the section, paint slip onto the gold piece, and replace it.

In **Figure 28**, a silver ball has fallen out. Enlarge the hole slightly with a small drill bit, paint the ball stem with slip, and replace the ball.

These examples should give you a good idea of what to do if things go wrong. PMC is very easy to fix.

The pieces are now ready to fire in the kiln (**Figure 29**). Review the following checklist to make sure that all the steps have been completed.

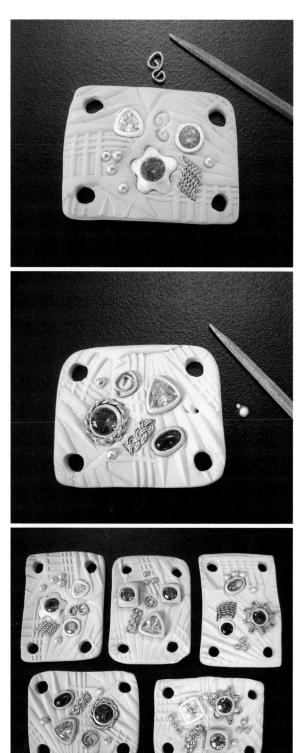

Figure 27
The curlicue has fallen out.

Figure 28
The ball has fallen out.

Figure 29
Pieces ready to fire.

CHECKLIST BEFORE FIRING THE BRACELET

PMC should be completely dry.

Use a small round file to clean out the corner holes and make them round. Keep in mind that original PMC will shrink about 25% when fired, so make the corner holes somewhat larger than you want them to be after firing.

Use 400- or 320-grit sandpaper to clean, smooth, and flatten the section backs. Also smooth all sharp edges and corners.

Use a needle to remove loose clay around all gem edges.

Clean all gemstones front and back with a dampened paintbrush to remove loose clay.

FIRING AND FINISHING

When all the sections are to your liking, fire them for two hours at 1650°F (900°C). Turn off the kiln and let the sections cool to room temperature before you remove them. Rushing the cooling process can result in stones broken by thermal stress.

After the sections have cooled, tumble four to six hours or overnight.

To make the connecting links, cut 1" (2.5 cm) lengths of half-hard, half-round 14-gauge (1.63 mm) sterling silver wire and file each end smooth. Use the middle section of your chain-nose pliers to roll each end toward the center. Reopen the links to insert them into the linking holes on the bracelet sections and reclose (**Figure 62**).

Attach two pairs of jump rings to two links joined to one end of the bracelet. Attach the clasp to the last two jump rings. The toggle catch is connected with two links joined to the other end of the bracelet.

You're finished! Now spend some time thinking of new ways to make a bracelet. You could make circular or oval sections. You could use jump rings instead of links, or maybe make a totally original clasp out of PMC. How about putting links on the back of the sections and having the sections overlap each other? There are many, many possibilities. We hope you enjoy this bracelet and have fun thinking of new ways to make more.

Figure 62
Steps in forming section links.

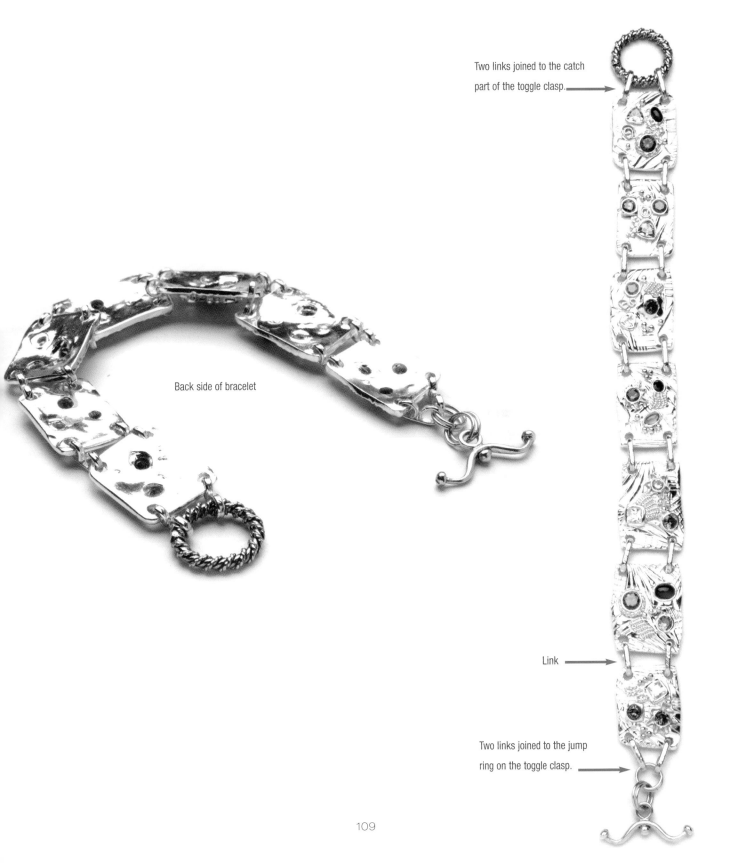

Two links joined to the catch part of the toggle clasp.

Back side of bracelet

Link

Two links joined to the jump ring on the toggle clasp.

blossom pendant for the woven neckpiece

Name the greatest of inventions. "Accident."
—Mark Twain (1835–1910)

This elegant silver pendant is a perfect complement to the woven neckpiece in Chapter 7. We chose a blossom design for our pendant, but you can make virtually anything you wish. For example, you could duplicate the pattern of an antique button or sculpt your own creation. The method for creating the pendant is easy, and you may decide to make several different ones, not only for the woven neckpiece, but for another necklace or chain.

Materials	Tools	
2 oz. (56 g) polymer clay	PMC tools	Ruler
25 g PMC3 or 25 g regular PMC	Olive oil	Baby powder or corn starch
Medium solder	320- and 200-grit sandpaper	18-gauge (1.2-mm) copper or
Flux	Utility knife	soft iron wire
	Torch	Burnisher
	Long sewing needle	Paper clip
	Darning needle	Third hand
	Stepped/chain-nose pliers	

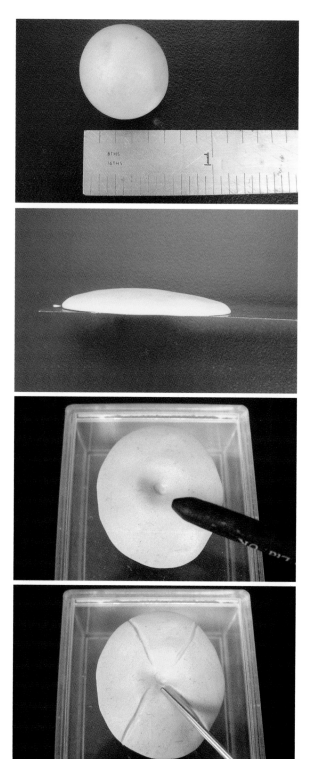

Figure 1
Polymer clay ball ½" (1.3 cm) in diameter.

Figure 2
Side view of flattened clay ball.

Figure 3
Make a dimple in the middle of the clay.

Figure 4
Make four grooves with a darning needle.

MAKING THE BLOSSOM MOLD

First we'll sculpt a blossom out of polymer clay, then use the blossom to make a negative mold. The negative mold will in turn be used to make the PMC blossom. We recommend Premo polymer clay for mold making. It's easy to work with, durable, and stays fairly flexible after baking. It should be available at your local hobby shop.

Cut a ½" (1.3 cm) square from the clay block. Knead the clay until it becomes malleable, then roll it into a ball about ½" (1.3 cm) in diameter (**Figure 1**).

Sprinkle a little baby powder or cornstarch on your work surface. Doing so will make the clay easy to pick up. (Formica is a good work surface for both PMC and polymer clay.)

Flatten the clay ball into a pancake shape about 1¼" (3.2 cm) in diameter. The pancake should be thick in the center and taper toward the edges (**Figure 2**).

Use a pencil eraser or any blunt object to make an indentation in the middle of the clay (**Figure 3**). Make four grooves in the clay with a darning needle (**Figure 4**).

Cut and remove pieces of clay from the edges to form the petals (**Figure 5**). When you are pleased with the shape, retaper and smooth the edges with your thumb or a piece of craft foam (**Figure 6**).

If you lose the center indentation and the grooves you made earlier, go back and reshape them (**Figure 7**). With a long sewing needle, score a series of fine lines radiating from the center of the blossom (**Figure 8**).

To make stamens for the blossom, cut four pieces of 18-gauge (1.02 mm) wire (copper or iron) ⅝" (1.5 cm) long. Bend ⅛" (3 mm) of each wire at a 90° angle (**Figure 9**). Curve the wires so they will rest snugly in the grooves. Insert the ⅛" (3 mm) bends into the center of the blossom (**Figure 10**).

Figure 5
Cut segments from the edges of the clay.

Figure 6
Retaper and smooth the edges.

Figure 7
Reshape the center indentation and the grooves.

Figure 8
Adding more lines to the blossom.

Figure 9
Wire stamens with one end at a 90° angle.

Figure 10
Wire stamens inserted into the blossom center and resting in the grooves.

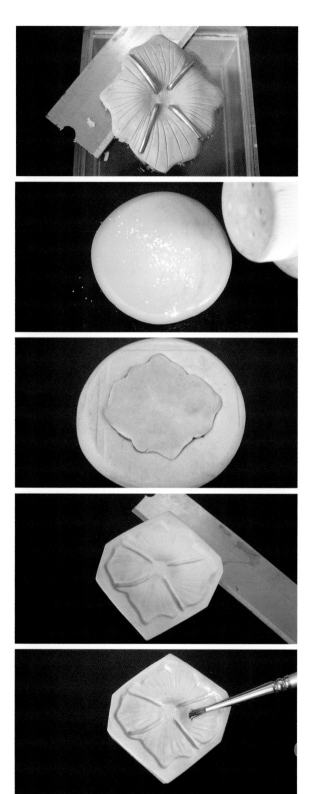

Figure 11
Lift the blossom with a tissue knife.

Figure 12
Lightly powder the soft clay.

Figure 13
Press the baked clay blossom face-down into the soft clay.

Figure 14
The trimmed negative mold.

Figure 15
Paint the baked negative mold with olive oil.

To lift the blossom off your work surface, slide a tissue knife under the clay and gently work beneath the edges until you reach the middle (**Figure 11**). Place the clay blossom on a piece of aluminum foil and bake in your kitchen oven at 275°F (135°C) for twenty minutes.

We'll use the baked clay blossom to make a negative mold. Take the polymer clay that is left in the 2-ounce (56-g) package, knead it until it's soft, and roll it into a ball. Press the clay ball onto the powdered work surface and flatten until it is about ½" (1.3 cm) thick.

Sprinkle a little powder on the soft clay (**Figure 12**). Press the baked clay blossom evenly into the soft clay about ¼" (6 mm) deep (**Figure 13**). Use a paper clip to gently pry up the baked clay until it releases from the soft clay (which is now the negative mold).

Cut off some of the excess soft clay with a tissue knife, leaving just a small border around the mold (**Figure 14**). Let the clay rest for five to ten minutes to regain some firmness.

Gently lift the negative mold with the tissue knife, place it on foil, and bake at 275°F (135°C) for twenty minutes. After the negative mold has cooled, lightly paint it with olive oil (**Figure 15**).

MAKING THE PMC BLOSSOM

Using your best guess, pinch off a piece of PMC big
enough to fill the mold (**Figure 16**). Don't worry
about getting the proper amount of PMC on the
first try. We never get it right the first time either!

Figure 17 shows that we need to add more PMC.
Remove the PMC from the mold and add more to
the mass. Oil your hands lightly with olive oil.
Knead the pieces of PMC until they are thoroughly
combined, then roll the clay into a smooth ball. The
PMC should be uniform, with no lines or creases.

With your thumb, press the PMC into the mold and
push it down and out toward the edges of the mold.
Continue to push the clay back and forth around
the edges until it's evenly pressed into the mold.
The PMC should be even with the top of the mold
(**Figure 18**). Use a tissue knife or a sturdy straight-
edged tool to scrape off any excess PMC. Let the
piece dry in the mold for at least a day.

The blossom should fall out of the mold very easily. If
the blossom doesn't fall out, give the mold a light
tap against a table. Be careful to catch the blossom
in your hand to reduce the risk of breakage. Allow
the freed blossom to dry for at least two more
hours. (Remember to place any extra PMC back in
its bag, or store it in water to make slip.)

Clean rough edges with sandpaper. Use a darning
needle to emphasize any lines on the blossom that
may have blurred during the molding process
(**Figure 19**).

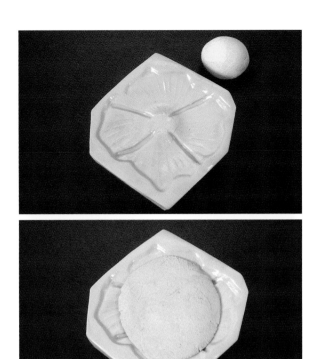

Figure 16
Pinch off a
piece of PMC
big enough to fit
inside the mold.

Figure 17
Press the PMC
into the mold.
Oops, not
enough PMC!

Figure 18
The PMC
pressed into
the mold.

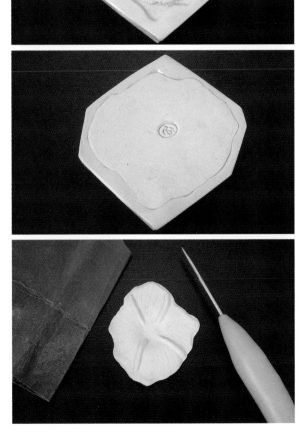

Figure 19
Reshape any
lines that have
become dull.

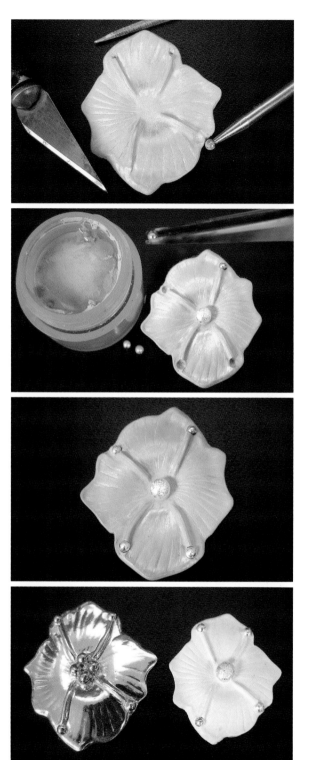

Figure 20
Cut off about ¹⁄₁₆" (2 mm) of the outer end of each stamen.

Figure 21
Dip each ball into PMC slip.

Figure 22
Balls on the end of each stamen and in the blossom center attached.

Figure 23
Left: PMC3 blossom. Right: Regular PMC blossom. (See text.)

Cut off about ¹⁄₁₆" (2 mm) of the outer end of each stamen with a utility knife, being careful not to cut into the blossom. Make a depression at the end of each cut-off stamen with a drill bit or round bur (**Figure 20**). These depressions will hold small decorative balls.

Roll four very small balls of PMC for the ends of the stamens and one larger ball for the middle of the blossom. Let them dry.

After the balls are dry, pick up one with tweezers, dip it in some PMC slip, and place it in a depression. Repeat with each small ball and the larger ball in the center of the blossom (**Figures 21 and 22**). If necessary, enlarge the depressions to fit the balls.

Allow the slip to dry, then turn the blossom upside down. If the balls don't fall out, they are attached firmly enough to fire in the kiln. If a ball *does* fall out, add more slip, let dry, and try again.

Once the blossom is completely dry, fire it at the recommended temperature and time for the type of PMC you have used. Allow it to cool to room temperature and place it in the tumbler for several hours. **Figure 23** shows a fired blossom made of PMC3 with 18k yellow gold balls in the center. This piece has been tumbled. The blossom on the right is made with regular PMC and has been fired but not tumbled. Both blossoms came from the same mold. Notice the difference in shrinkage between PMC3 and original PMC. You can also see why tumbling PMC after firing is so necessary.

ATTACHING THE BAIL

We have chosen a piece of sterling silver patterned wire for the bail. You can also use double half-round or other sturdy, heavy-gauge silver wire. The end that will be soldered to the back of the blossom must be filed perfectly flat.

PMC is much more porous than sheet metal. During firing the burning off of binders that help make the clay leaves tiny holes in the metal. These holes must be compressed as much as possible in order for the blossom to be soldered. Compress the back of the blossom with a burnisher. Use lots of pressure and give the back a mirror shine. If your soldering job fails, you probably have not burnished enough.

Use a third hand to hold the bail (**Figure 24**). Place the blossom facedown and level in a nest of charcoal block (**Figure 25**). The charcoal will keep the blossom steady and help retain heat.

Flux the back of the blossom and the end of the bail that is to be soldered. Line up the third hand with the blossom and lower the bail into place (**Figure 26**). Make sure the bail is straight and even and in good contact with the blossom. Place solder chips on the blossom against the bail.

Apply the torch to the area surrounding the blossom first, then gradually heat the blossom itself. The solder will turn brown, then white, then clear. At this point, concentrate more heat on the bail and the area to be soldered. When the solder flows, remove the torch. **Figure 27** shows the soldered bail.

Figure 24
Third hand holding the bail.

Figure 25
Blossom in nest of charcoal.

Figure 26
Third hand holding bail in place.

Figure 27
The soldered bail.

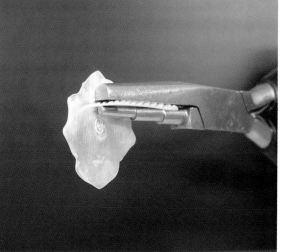

Figure 28
Hold the bail close to the join.

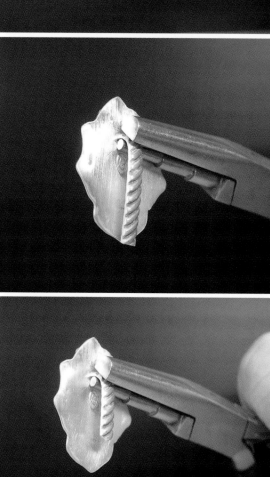

Figure 29
Bend the bail downward with your free hand.

Figure 30
Bail trimmed and smoothed.

Grasp the bail as closely as possible to the blossom with the smallest part of your stepped/chain-nose pliers (Figure 28). With your free hand, bend the bail down over the pliers until it is very close to the blossom (Figure 29), being careful not to apply force against the soldered join.

In this case, we have made the bail a little too long, so we'll cut off about ¼" (6 mm) and file the end smooth (Figure 30).

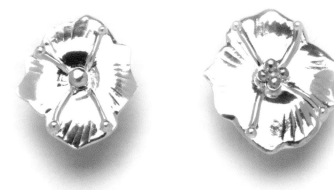

If there is fire scale on the pendant, place it in the pickle pot, rinse, and put the piece in the tumbler.

You're finished! Now that you know how to make molds, we hope that you will come up with many different ideas for pendants and other projects. Enjoy!

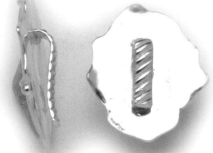

GALLERY

resources

RIO GRANDE (THE BELL GROUP)
www.riogrande.com
(800) 545-6566
(800) 965-2329 Fax
(800) 253-9738 Telephone for Canada, Virgin Islands, and Puerto Rico
(505) 839-3011 Telephone for all other countries
(505) 839-3016 Fax for all other countries
7500 Bluewater Road NW
Albuquerque, NM 87121-1962
Specialties: Tools and equipment, materials, display products, and refining.

RISHASHAY
www.rishashay.com
(800) 517-3311
(406) 549-3467 Fax
inquire@rishashay.com
PO Box 8271
Missoula, MT 59807
Specialties: Bali beads, clasps, bead caps, and finished jewelry.

ROSS METALS
www.rossmetals.com
(800) 654-7677
(212) 768-3018
54 West 47th Street
New York, NY 10036
Specialties: Patterned wire, alloys, wire, sheet metal, ready-made castings, mountings, charms, wedding sets, and refining.

Web Sites

WWW.ART-CLAY.COM
Similar to Art Clay World, with helpful information and contests.

WWW.ARTCLAYWORLD.COM
A site for another form of Precious Metal Clay called Art Clay, lots of good information on this new jewelry medium.

WWW.BALI-SILVER-BEADS.COM/DEFAULT.HTM
Bali beads direct from Bali.

WWW.DICHROICLADY.COM
The website of Carolyn Beebe, The Dichroic Lady, who makes dichroic glass that resembles black opal. The stones in the book were made by Carolyn. While we use many of her cabochons, the glass is available in other forms.

WWW.DICHROICPATTERNS.COM
This site sells dichroic glass and an interesting kind of decal for jewelry.

WWW.GANOKSIN.COM
Lurk and learn as some of the most prominent people in the jewelry business discuss every aspect of jewelry making. When you feel brave enough, put your question(s) before this group of experts. Beginners' questions are answered clearly and generously.

Ganoksin also has galleries of members' work as well as an extensive library of topics. Metalcalc can help you with any mathematical formulae or conversion.

WWW.JEWELRYMAKING.ABOUT.COM
This site has projects and technical information related to jewelry making.

WWW.JEWELRYTOOLSBYMILAND.COM
If you can't find a specialty tool anywhere else, look here. If you still can't find what you need, this gentleman will probably make it for you.

WWW.LAPIDARYART.COM
Amy O'Connell's website. Jewelry plus tutorials on lapidary, jewelry, and photography.

WWW.LAPIDARYJOURNAL.COM/
TECH_HOME.CFM
Lapidary Journal magazine's website with lots of projects and technical information.

WWW.MONSTERSLAYER.COM
No print catalog, but lots of supplies, tools, materials, sterling and fine silver findings, beads, equipment, and display items.

WWW.PMCCONNECTION.COM
A good PMC site.

WWW.PMCGUILD.COM/NEWSFRAMES.HTML
This site has locations and times for lessons, supplies, techniques, and galleries for the PMC enthusiast.

WWW.SNAGMETALSMITH.ORG/SNAG/LINKS
Useful links provided by the highly respected SNAG organization.

Books

Brephol, Dr. Erhard. *The Theory & Practice of Goldsmithing*. Portland, Maine: Brynmorgen Press, 2001.

Codina, Carles. *The Complete Book of Jewelry Making*. Asheville, North Carolina: Lark Books, 2000.

Finegold, Rupert, and William Seitz. *Silversmithing*. Iola, Wisconsin: Krause Publications, 1983.

Fisch, Arline M. *Textile Techniques in Metal*. Asheville, North Carolina: Lark Books, 2003.

McCreight, Tim. *The Complete Metalsmith*. New York: Sterling Publishing, 1991.

———. *Working with Precious Metal Clay*. Portland, Maine: Brynmorgen Press, 2000.

McGrath, Jinks. *The Encyclopedia of Jewelry Making Techniques*. Philadelphia: Running Press, 2003.

Revere, Alan. *The Art of Jewelry Making: Classic & Original Designs*. New York: Sterling Publishing, 2001.

———. *Professional Goldsmithing: A Contemporary Guide to Traditional Jewelry*. Revere Academy Books, 1991.

Untracht, Oppi. *Jewelry: Concepts and Technology*. North Pomfret, Vermont: Trafalgar Square Books, 1996.

Von Neumann, Robert. *The Design and Creation of Jewelry*. Iola, Wisconsin: Krause Publications, 2003.

Wicks, Sylvia. *Jewelry Making Manual*. Chartwell House, 1989.

Wire, CeCe. *Creative Metal Clay Jewelry: Techniques, Projects, Inspiration*. Asheville, North Carolina: Lark Books, 2003.

Magazines

Bead & Button
www.beadandbutton.com

Beadwork
www.interweave.com/bead/default.asp

Colored Stone
www.colored-stone.com

The Crafts Report
www.craftsreport.com

Jewelry Crafts
www.amazon.com

Lapidary Journal
www.lapidaryjournal.com

Metalsmith
www.snagmetalsmith.org/metalsmith/default.asp

Ornament
Call (760) 599-0222 or
Fax (760) 559-0228

Rock & Gem
www.rockngem.com/home.shtml

The Sunshine Artist
www.sunshineartist.com
Show and gallery schedules.

index